THIS IS THE DAY THAT THE LORD HAS MADE

A DAILY DEVOTIONAL

Author:
Nykole Wyatt
In collaboration with her mother
Faye DeWalt

Copyright © 2014 Kole's Konsulting Nykole Wyatt All Rights Reserved

No part of this book may be reproduced in any form without the expressed written permission from the publisher or author, except in the case of brief quotation embodied in critical articles or reviews.

All scriptures quotations, are taken from the Holy Bible, King James®, New King James ®, NIV, ® and The Message®.

ISBN: 0692239324
ISBN-13: 978-0-692-23932-2

Jackie,

I wanted to bless you with a copy of my book in hopes that each day gives you a renewed perspective for what God has planned for you.

Always,
Nikol
9-11-2020

Acknowledgements and Dedication

We thank God, our heavenly father, from which all blessings flow. We thank those who have been supportive of this project. We thank those who have pushed and stood as our accountability partners on this project.
We thank our family. We thank our friends.
We believe that every day should begin with prayer and a devotion to God. We have developed this devotional to help you each day.

This daily devotional is dedicated to our loved one, whom has gone on to glory. May your soul rest, reside, and rule with our Lord and Savior Jesus Christ forever more.
Joshua Michael Wyatt
May 5, 1987-November 24, 2010

DAY 1

✠

Proverbs 12:2 "A good man obtains favor from the Lord, but a man of wicked intentions He will condemn."

Today, and every day, you must be your best. Strive for excellence in everything that you do. The Lord shows favor to those who are good and seek excellence. Those who think of plans of devastation and evil ways put a frown on the Lord's face. He disapproves of those actions. You are a good man or woman. Show God your goodness by showing your goodness to all around you.

DAY 2

✠

Psalm 31:3-5 "For you are my rock and my fortress: Therefore, for your name's sake, lead me and guide me. Pull me out of the net which they have secretly laid for me, for You are my strength. Into your hand I commit my spirit: You have redeemed me. O Lord God of truth."

Today may be one of those days where you question everything. Know now that God is your rock. He will lead you, guide you and keep you, even though there may be some who secretly plot against you. Where there is good there is also evil. Know that He is your strength today and always.

DAY 3

✟

Isaiah 40:31 "But those who wait on the Lord shall renew their strength: They shall mount up on wings like eagles, they shall run and not be weary, and they shall walk and not faint."

Today, the wait is worth it. It doesn't matter why you wait or even how long you wait. With God by your side, the wait renews you. With renewed strength you can have anything and be anything. The choice is yours. You must always reverence in the waiting period because good things really do come to those who wait.

DAY 4

✝

2 Timothy 2:15-15 "Be diligent to present yourself approved to God, a worker who does not need to be ashamed, rightly dividing the word of truth. But shun profane and idle babblings, for they will increase to more ungodliness."

Today, whatever you decide to do, do it with the best of your abilities. Speak with intelligence and understanding. Stay away from idle gossip. God does not approve of it. Gossip leads nowhere and the purpose of today is for you to achieve your goals and get somewhere. Get to where God wants you to be and to where He would have you to be. Study God's word and He will show you where you should be in His word.

DAY 5

✝

1 Peter 5:6-11 "Therefore humble yourselves under the mighty hand of God, that He may exalt you in due time, casting all your cares upon him, for He cares for you. Be sober, be vigilant: because your adversary the devil walks about like a roaring lion seeking whom he may devour. Resist him, steadfast in the faith, knowing that the same sufferings are experienced by your brotherhood in the world. But may the God of all grace, who called us to his eternal glory by Christ Jesus, after you have suffered a while, perfect, establish, strengthen, and settle you. To him be the glory and dominion forever and ever. Amen."

Today, this week, this month, this year, at some point, the enemy will come after you. The enemy lies in wait for the opportunity to see you struggle, miss out or simply mess up. Disguised in many ways, this enemy could be a family member, co-worker or trusted friend. Never mind who they are. Never mind when they will begin their plot against you. Just know that God is with you always. Cast your thoughts, cares, and trust in Him.

DAY 6

✝

Genesis 1: 31 "Then God saw everything that He had made, and indeed it was very good. So the evening and the morning were the sixth day"

Today, remember everything that God made is good. That includes you. Start each day by telling yourself this. Reinforce this into yourself. Put this in your mind and believe it. Tell yourself, "everything God made is good and I am good." This affirming confirmation will reinforce the good of God and the good that you are.

DAY 7

✝

Philippians 4:19 "And my God shall supply all your need according to His riches in glory by Christ Jesus."

Today, whatever you need, God's got it. Remember those simple words. Cast all of your cares upon our Lord. Go to God in prayer with your wants and your needs and God will supply.

DAY 8

✞

Romans 10:17 "So then faith comes by hearing, and hearing by the word of God."

Today, you may be tested. In order to have faith that God will see you through, you must know the word of God. The only way to know it is to hear it. I challenge you today to read the bible out loud or buy the bible on CD and listen to it in your car. Relish in ministry teachings by audio or by reading them aloud. There is something about hearing the word of God aloud and speaking those words into the atmosphere that will begin to shift things in your favor.

DAY 9

✞

James 5:16 "Confess your trespasses to one another, and pray for one another, that ye may be healed. The effectual fervent prayer of a righteous man avails much."

Today is the day of forgiveness. Tell your friend of any wrong doings or vices you have. Tell them what you have done wrong. Take today to begin to make things right. Do not leave today without taking the step to make things right and ensure you are on a path of rebuilding. Then take a moment to pray. Pray with your friend. When you pray, ask for a forgiving heart and a right mind. This will be needed in the days ahead.

DAY 10

✟

Philippians 4:6-7 "Be anxious for nothing, but in everything by prayer and supplication, with thanksgiving, let your requests be made known to God; and the peace of God, which surpasses all understanding, will guard your hearts and minds through Christ Jesus."

Today, when you pray to the Lord, begin with thanks. Be thankful before asking God for the things that you want. Remember, no matter what you ask for, God will provide it. With Jesus Christ, God will protect what matters most and that includes your heart. In everything that you do today and every day, give thanks.

DAY 11

✞

Joshua 1:9 "Have I not commanded you? Be strong and of good courage; do not be afraid, nor be dismayed, for the Lord your God is with you wherever you go."

Today, stand still and listen. Be strong. Know that God is with you. Today's obstacle may be one that will discourage you, sadden you or cause you to have fear. Remember fear is only false expectations appearing real. Sadness comes and goes, and discouragement is a temporary feeling. God is always with you and He will never leave you. Focus on that when the obstacles, issues, or enemy tries to come at you. Focus on that when distractions come your way. Be strong and stay encouraged.

DAY 12

✞

Genesis 1:27 "So God created man in His own image, in the image of God, He created him; male and female, He created them."

Today, know that you were created in the image of God. Male or female, you were created in God's own likeness. You must always know that your physical image is perfect in Him. You were created as God would have you to be. Your eyes that may be spaced a little far apart, your nose that may be smaller than most, your lips that may be fuller than most, all of you from your head to your precious toes, was created in God's image. God's image is perfect. So then you are perfect in God's eyes. Accept it. Relish in it. Love it and live it. It is you. It is not anyone else. Since it is you, go and enjoy you. Look at yourself in the mirror, smile and enjoy what God has created, you.

DAY 13

✞

John 1:5 "And the light shines in the darkness, and the darkness did not comprehend (or overcome) it"

Today, you are the light that shines in the darkness. People will not understand why others are drawn to you. People will try to move the masses away from you because you have this natural ability to be the light. But understand that light you possess is Jesus Christ shining through. Remember that in everything that you do. Jesus will see you through it all, even the dark times because He is the light that will also guide you.

DAY 14

✝

Galatians 6:9 "And let us not be weary in well doing: for in due season we shall reap, if we faint not."

Today, you are doing well. You have been sowing seeds of the goodness that you are. Do not let discouragements put a damper on your good deeds. Do not let jealousy, strife, or half-heartedness be the reason you do not reap the rewards of your good deeds. Stay focused on the goodness that is you. Stay focused on the goodness that you do. Do not give up. If you do not give up the goodness, in God's time, you will reap the benefits of your good deeds. Remember, you live to please the Lord. Everything that you do is to please our heavenly father. When He is put first in all the things that you do, you bring a smile to his face. So do not get down and out with misery. Realize that because time is on your side. God will give you the desires of your heart if you do not give up. Do everything with gladness and with joy. This proves you are a true server of the Lord, and for that, He will reward your goodness here on earth, as well as in heaven.

DAY 15

✟

Matthews 10:32-33 "If you tell others that you belong to me, I will tell my Father in heaven that you are my followers. But if you reject me, I will tell my Father in Heaven that you don't belong to me."

Today, everyone wants to belong with someone or to something. That is why people join organizations, fraternities, sororities, clubs and even cliques. Even on a job one may want a sense of belonging. Look at it this way: if everyone is going out to lunch and they don't invite you, most people will begin to feel some type of way about the situation. That is simply the innate need to belong. Jesus said "you belong to me". Share that with the world and he will not deny you in front of God. No matter what the obstacle, not matter what the triumph, at the end of the day you belong to Jesus. He is your Lord and Savior. As such, be proud that Jesus has accepted you unconditionally. Since you have been accepted without regard to the size of your hips, or the bulge of your biceps, accept Jesus and let people know whom you belong to, our Lord and Savior Jesus Christ.

DAY 16

✝

Proverbs 11:25 "The generous soul will be made rich, and he who waters will also be watered himself."

Today is about giving. It's about understanding that you must give in order to receive everything that you want. The best way to look at this is to give, give and give your way to success. Give your way to everything. Give your way to financial freedom. Give your way to the best life you can ever have. Your gift can be tangible or intangible. From this day forward, live each day on purpose and with the purpose of giving. Give of your time. Reach out to someone, anyone. Reach out with your hand, your voice and your heart. Begin today and each day with the intent to give more than you did yesterday.

DAY 17

✝

Proverbs 18:22 "He who finds a wife finds a good thing, and obtains favor from the Lord."

Today, I offer to expand on this scripture just a bit. This scripture is so often misused and misunderstood. What must be understood is the scripture references a love that must be present that is without a doubt unconditional or what is commonly referred to as agape love. A man that has the ability to feel agape love toward a woman and she in-turn is able to reciprocate, then he has found his wife. In finding his wife, he has then found a good thing and with such a good thing he obtains favor from the Lord. The key is that agape love.

DAY 18

✝

Jeremiah 1:5 "Before I shaped you in the womb, I knew all about you. Before you saw the light of day, I had holy plans for you: A prophet to the nations, that's what I had in mind for you."

Today, don't worry about the things that you feel may not be right with you. Remember, God knew you before you were even born. He knew you were going to have abs of steel or flabs and no steel. He knew every strand of hair on your head. He knew you would need braces or have a birth mark. He knew who you were before you were you. The best part is he loves you anyway. He loves the quirkiness about you. He loves the confidence you have. He loves when you are embarrassed. He even loves when you show your vulnerable side. Never forget that love, it is unconditional.

DAY 19

✝

Jeremiah 29:11 "For I know the thoughts I think toward you, says the LORD, thoughts of peace and not evil, to give you a future and a hope."

Today, remember that God is thinking of you always. Those thoughts do not come with any negativity. He has hope for you and your future. He only wants the best for you. Peace, goodness, and prosperity, not evil or negativity. Remember this when you are faced with a tough decision today. God wants you to have a future, but you have to want it too.

DAY 20

✝

Matthew 4:4 "But He answered and said, 'It is written, "Man shall not live by bread alone, but by every word that proceeds from the mouth of God.'"

Today, the word of God is here to feed you spiritually, three hundred sixty five days a year. Day after day, and month after month the word is here. You eat food for nourishment of your body. You drink water to sustain your body. You read the word of God to nourish and sustain your body spiritually and mentally. Enjoy God's word today and everyday.

DAY 21

✟

Matthew 5:16 "In the same way, let your light shine before others, that they may see your good deeds and glorify your Father in heaven."

Today, know that the God in you is the God everyone should see. When people see you, and interact with you, there should not be a question as to who is the head of your life. God is not someone or something that should be hidden from those that know you. In fact He is the secret that can't and shouldn't be kept a secret.

DAY 22

✟

Matthew 6:33 "But seek first the kingdom of God and His righteousness, and all these things shall be added to you."

Today, before you make a big decision, before you make a little decision, before you do anything that will affect those around you, look toward heaven for your guidance. Everything that you want will come if you go after those things that are pleasing to God. In every single thing that you do, you must put God first.

DAY 23

✝

Leviticus 26:12 "I will walk among you and be your God, and you shall be my people."

Today, God will not leave you. He is always with you, walking with you and guiding you. Know that he is your God. He is your heavenly father. He is family and a great figure in your life. So start your day with the knowledge that God is here and not going anywhere. He will not leave you. Even when you feel like things are not going your way, remember God is still here. Just reach out to Him and just lean on Him. He will have your back of you let him.

DAY 24

✞

Proverbs 18:10 "The name of the Lord is a strong tower: the righteous runneth into it, and is safe."

Today, when you go out into the world, when you begin this day, remember that the Lord is your strength. You can run to Him for anything. You can run to Him for everything. The Lord is a safe haven, even in the midst of the darkest and most unforeseen events.

DAY 25

✠

John 10:10 "The thief does not come except to steal, and to kill and to destroy. I have come that they may have life, and that they may have it more abundantly."

Today, know what you have, and that's an abundant life. The enemy does not want you to have abundance. He wants to destroy you and everything you have. Be wise about the people that you surround yourself with. Surround yourself with those people that will fight spiritually with you. Those people that want what you want; people with like minds, like hearts and like spirits. The enemy will not be supportive of your efforts. The enemy will not be supportive of the good that God has for you. He will try to destroy it all. Remember that as you encounter people, there will be those in your life that don't appear to be what they say they are. Everyone that is in your life is not for you. Just know that God is for you. Know that with Him, it does not matter who then is against you.

DAY 26

✟

Romans 5:8 "But God demonstrates His own love toward us, in that while we were still sinners, Christ died for us."

Today, I want you to take a few moments and really think about the scripture of choice. There is no greater act of love than sacrifice. Jesus Christ, Son of God, died for you. He died for us. It can be very overwhelming to know such love as this. I urge you to be thankful that you have chosen salvation. This choice was given to you as a part of the sacrifice that Jesus made.

DAY 27

✞

Romans 12:2 "Do not be conformed to this world, but be transformed by the renewing of your mind, that you may prove what is that good and acceptable and perfect will of God."

Today, and every single day, take everything that you are comprised of and give it to God. Focus that energy towards God. God does not want you to walk around this world mirroring and shadowing what is acceptable. He wants you to be successful. He wants you to set yourself apart from everyone else. You can do this by keeping God at your side. He wants you to be the shining light that everyone flocks to. He doesn't want you running after anything that is not of Him.

DAY 28

✝

James 1:19 "My dear brothers and sisters, take note of this: Everyone should be quick to listen, slow to speak and slow to become angry."

Today, as you begin your day, remember to listen. Listen before you speak ad before you react. Then when you speak, do not speak with anger. Today may be the day that you are really put to the test. Trials and tribulations are only tests to ensure you have a testimony. Sometime you have to go through to get too. Whatever the lesson that presents itself to you today, be sure you listen. Be sure you move without anger and with acceptance. Choose your reactions and your words wisely.

DAY 29

✝

Philippians 1:6 "Being confident of this very thing, that He who has begun a good work in you will complete it until the day of Jesus Christ."

Today, God has done a great work in you. Remember He created you. Everything about you is perfect in the eyes of God. He knew you before you were born and he has begun a good work within you. Be confident as you go out into the world that God will keep you. You are a person that is "a good work", and a producer of good work.

DAY 30

✝

Ephesians 4:31 "Get rid of all bitterness, rage and anger, brawling and slander, along with every form of malice."

Today, you may be going through some serious issues. People are saying things and doing things to bring your character in question. Regardless of what others have done to you, God wants you to get rid of the hatred you harbor in your heart toward anyone or anything. Holding on to negative feelings adds undue stress to your overall health. Your body is your temple. This includes your mind and your feelings all need much care. Leave the anger alone. Leave filth out of your mouth. Strive for excellence and all things positive to reinforce the goodness of the Lord.

DAY 31

✝

Colossians 3:23 "And whatever you do, do it heartily, as to the Lord and not to man."

Today, and every day, you must put God first in everything that you do. He is the light that shines within you. God wants you to put him first. When you go to work, to the gym, to the school, no matter what, ensure God is at the forefront of everything that you do.

DAY 32

✝

Hebrews 4:12 "God means what he says. What he says goes. His powerful Word is sharp as a surgeon's scalpel, cutting through everything, whether doubt or defense, laying us open to listen and obey. Nothing and no one is impervious to God's Word. We can't get away from it—no matter what."

Today, God's word is here to stay. It is here to be a guide to us all in this race through life. We heed to God's word. God's word is all around. You cannot get away from it. Embrace the word. Use the word. Let the word be instrumental in everything that you do. God's word is a powerful weapon against anything not of God. God's word is here to stay. Incorporate it into your life. Let it guide you. Let it be the everything that it is...**B**asic **I**nstructions **B**efore **L**eaving **E**arth...the **BIBLE**.

DAY 33

✟

1 Thessalonians 5:11 "Therefore encourage one another and build each other up, just as in fact you are doing."

Today, nothing feels better than when someone encourages you. Return the feeling by encouraging someone else. There are some that do that anything, continue to do so. God sees this. Be that one that encourages a person to go for that big promotion, or stick to that weight loss program. Encourage them to live a better life. When you encourage others you also encourage yourself.

DAY 34

✝

Hebrews 13:6 "So we may boldly say: 'The LORD is my helper; I will not fear. What can man do to me?"

Today, know that the Lord is with you. There is nothing that you should fear. You should not fear unemployment. You should not fear a cancelled event. You should not fear the stock market or an economic depression. What must resonate with you is that the Lord is here to help guide you and keep you. There is nothing that anyone can do to you that the Lord cannot fix. Tell your enemies to try their best. You have the Lord on your side and they will not win.

DAY 35

✝

1 Peter 5:8 "Stay alert! Watch out for your great enemy, the devil. He prowls around like a roaring lion, looking for someone to devour."

Today, you may meet a person that will make you feel like you have to watch them. This person may make you feel unsure about something or someone else. Today, you must stay alert! The enemy uses others people to deceive you. Sometimes you may not be aware are sitting and plotting against you and everything that you stand for. Be cautious about whom ever you surround yourself with.

DAY 36

✞

Matthews 6: 2-4 "So when you give to the needy, do not announce it with trumpets, as the hypocrites do in the synagogues and on the streets, to be honored by others. Truly I tell you, they have received their reward in full. But when you give to the needy, do not let your left hand know what your right hand is doing, so that your giving may be in secret. Then your Father, who sees what is done in secret, will reward you."

Today, and every day, know that God is watching you. It does not matter if anyone else can see you. When you are doing good deeds, or good work, it will shows in your work. Remember that putting God first is what God wants to see. If you are doing the work as to please God, then ultimately you will please others. Just know this, don't do good to get applause or some type of acknowledgement from those around you. Do it because God sees you and he comes first in everything that you do.

DAY 37

✝

Hebrews 13: 8 "Jesus Christ is the same yesterday, today, and forever."

Today, know that Jesus has not changed from the person He was yesterday. He will not change from the person He will be tomorrow. He is not like some of the people in our lives who change as the wind blows or as often as they change clothes. Often times, those changes are not good changes anyway. Jesus is the one irrefutable constant in your life. No matter what the situation is, Jesus will still be there, just like He was yesterday, just like He is today, and just like He will be tomorrow. Don't ever doubt that Jesus Christ is the same.

DAY 38

✝

Proverbs 25: 21-22 "If your enemy is hungry, give him food! If he is thirsty, give him something to drink! This will make him feel ashamed of himself, and God will reward you."

Today, even though you have enemies, still treat them good. Treat them as if they are not your enemy. Treat them like they are indeed friends. When you treat your enemies with a kind heart, God is pleased. Nothing can be more rewarding than knowing that God is pleased. This gives more meaning to the "Golden Rule" of treating others the way you want to be treated.

DAY 39

✝

Proverbs 13:9 "The light of the righteous shines brightly, but the lamp of the wicked is snuffed out."

Today, the light of the Lord shines brightly through you. Evil, wicked, negative people live in the darkness. Remember, don't let that darkness get to you. Keep your light that shines within, shining bright. You can lead anyone out of darkness and into the light if you just believe.

DAY 40

✟

Proverbs 17:22 "A cheerful heart is good medicine, but a broken spirit saps a person's strength."

Today, like big part of each day relies heavily on what weighs most on your heart. Begin today putting cheerful thoughts into your mind. You may be going through some hard times, but understand in order to survive you will need to put positivity at the forefront of everything that you do. When your heart is full of joy, keep it that way. Don't let others take your joy by putting those things that are negative in you.

DAY 41

✝

Romans 15:4 "These things that were written in the Scriptures so long ago are to teach us patience and to encourage us so that we will look forward expectantly to the time when God will conquer sin and death."

Today, remember that the scriptures and stories of the bible were written for you, for us. These scriptures are here to teach us, mold us, shape us, and guide us. Remember the words of the bible in your daily walk with God and in your physical walk in the world. Be like Christ every day. Do not be afraid to use the scriptures as your guide.

DAY 42

✝

Hebrew 13:5 "Keep your lives free from the love of money and be content with what you have, because God has said, "Never will I leave you; never will I forsake you."

Today, be content with the things that you have. Stop chasing after a dollar. Don't misunderstand me. You do have to work. However, you do not have to be obsessed with money. Remember, when you are wise with little, God will give you much.

DAY 43

✞

Hebrews 4:16 "Let us therefore come boldly to the throne of grace that we may obtain mercy, and find grace to help in time of need."

Today, when you come to the Lord, come with confidence. Know that God is here for you. Since He is here for you, you must come to Him standing and knowing that He will be there for you; knowing that He will listen to you, knowing that He will come through for you.

DAY 44

✝

Hebrews 11:6 "And it is impossible to please God without faith. Anyone who wants to come to him must believe that God exists and that he rewards those who sincerely seek him."

Today is not the time to have a lack of faith. If you are living each day as unto the Lord, then you cannot do it without faith. God is not pleased with lack of faith. Seek after Him and have faith in Him and everything that He stands for. He will direct your path.

DAY 45

✝

1 Peter 4:8 "And above all things have fervent love for one another, for 'love will cover a multitude of sins.'"

Today, at the end of the day, what matters is the love you show to everyone. Love truly does conquer all, including sins. We must have an uncompromising love for one another. A love that lives on beyond what we are right now. A love that teaches, that endures, that believes and conquers. That love will is the love of the Lord. That love has been demonstrated to you by the death of Jesus Christ on the cross. Sometimes it may seem overwhelming to know that someone has such a great love for you. Understand that having that true unconditional love is what has saved you and will save you from all things including your sins.

DAY 46

✝

Proverbs 16:3 "Commit your works to the Lord, and your thoughts will be established."

Today, everything that you do must be done unto the good of the Lord. Put God first in everything that you do. Once you do that, God will bring about the things you want. The will of God is reflected in what you do when you put Him first. God will be pleased because you are pleasing to Him. His will must then be pleasing to you in all things. Not just in your needs but in your wants too. Be committed to the God by putting him first.

DAY 47

☦

1 John 4:19 "We love him because He first loved us."

Today, know that before you were born, before your parents even thought to think of you, God loved you. He was the first person to love you. He loves you more than you could ever learn to love yourself. He loves you totally and completely. Remember that today and always. God loves you. He is faithful and just to keep His promise to us. There is no greater love than the love of God.

DAY 48

✝

1 Thessalonians 5:23 "Rejoice always, pray continually, give thanks in all circumstances; for this is God's will for you in Christ Jesus."

Today, as a Christian, know that the enemy is always at work. He wants to you in harm's way. He wants to take what is rightfully yours while making life more difficult. Remember that you serve a God that can do anything. He can take your problems and make them disappear. He can take you and raise you to be the leader you were meant to be. He can do whatever you ask him to do. So rejoice today. Rejoice with the knowledge that no matter what the enemy tries to bring your way, God has your back. God will come out on top placing you at the head and not the tale. Today is about you. Pray to God for whatever you want or need. Continue to rejoice in what He has already done and will continue to do. Expect the unexpected. Today is a new day!

DAY 49

✝

Luke 6:38 "Give, and it will be given to you. A good measure, pressed down, shaken together and running over, will be poured into your lap. For with the measure you use, it will be measured to you."

Today, give your best. When you give, you receive that back. If you give out bad and you will receive the bad in return. If you give out good you will also receive good back to you. The more you give, the more you receive. What will you do today to ensure your cup is full and overflowing with the things that you want and need? How much can you give to get what you really want? Put God in your giving and your rewards will be more than you expect.

DAY 50

✝

Psalm 1:3 "And he shall be like a tree planted by the rivers of water, that bringeth forth his fruit in his season; his leaf also shall not wither; and whatsoever he doeth shall prosper."

Today, whatever you do, remain firm in your convictions. Do not be easily moved or swayed from what you know is right. Do the right thing. Do not let friends change your mind or convince you that the wrong thing is the right thing when you know better.

DAY 51

✝

John 3:1 "For God so loved the world that He gave His only begotten Son, that whoever believes in Him should not perish but have everlasting life."

Today, know that God has shown us the ultimate act of love by sending his one and only son Jesus Christ t die for your sins. If you just believe and trust in the Lord you too shall have eternal life with Him. God wants you to know that your true life does not end with your death. Because you love the Lord and have chosen to serve Him, you will be rewarded. Putting God first in your life is all God asks. It is all He wants from you.

DAY 52

✞

Psalm 3:3 "And he shall be like a tree planted by the rivers of water, that bringeth forth his fruit in his season; his leaf also shall not wither; and whatsoever he doeth shall prosper."

Today, stand firm. Do not be moved. Don't let any obstacles that may come your way push you into a place that you have no business. You have to remember that everything in life is not good. And if you let your convictions and beliefs be swayed, you could lose everything. Hold on tightly to what you know is right. Do not be tricked, mocked, or persuaded to change what you know is right. Be firm and be unmovable just like a tree. Prosperity hangs in the balance. Your success lies in your ability to stand firm.

DAY 53

✝

Deuteronomy 31:6 "Be strong. Take courage. Don't be intimidated. Don't give them a second thought because GOD, your God, is striding ahead of you. He's right there with you. He won't let you down; he won't leave you."

Today may end up being one of those days. But know that God has your back. He is already looking out for you. Don't be tripped up. Don't let what others may be saying or doing get to you. The devil is really busy and so are his followers. But understand you must remain focused. God has so much for you and you cannot get distracted by that which is not of God. Remember the vision that He gave you. Remember your purpose. Focus on that because regardless of the attacks that you come under, God is there and will always be there.

DAY 54

✝

Psalm 27:11 "Teach me your way, O LORD, and lead me in a smooth path, because of my enemies."

Today, ask God to guide your path. Ask God to clear your path. Ask God to remove any obstacles that may come your way. Ask Him to help you overcome any obstacles that may come your way. Know that God is here for you despite your enemies. Despite anything contradictory, God is here for you.

DAY 55

✞

Psalm 32: 8 "I will instruct you and teach you in the way you should go; I will counsel you with my loving eye on you."

Today, God will give you the tools, insights and strategies needed for you to succeed. Those things may come through other individuals. Regardless of how it comes to you, He sends you what you need to be successful. He sends you what you need to get through. He sends you what you need to understand that everything that He has for you is for you. God's love for you is constantly on you and with you. Be receptive. Be ready. Everything is turning around in your favor. Stay focused and watch God work.

DAY 56

✝

Psalm 34:1-3 "I will bless the LORD at all times; His praise shall continually be in my mouth. My soul shall make its boast in the LORD; the humble shall hear of it and be glad. Oh, magnify the LORD with me, and let us exalt His name together."

Today, the Lord has blessed you with another day. Rejoice and be glad in it. Because you were given another day, the devil is mad. He only wants to trip you up today. Be on the lookout. Still rejoice in the Lord. Tell everyone how wonderful it is to be among the living. Share the goodness of the Lord with everyone.

DAY 57

✝

Proverbs 11:14 "Without good direction, people lose their way; the more wise counsel you follow, the better your chances."

Today, go to God for the things that you need. He will show you the way to go. He will answer your prayer requests and He will lead and guide you in that way that is pleasing, righteous, and good. When seeking advice outside of God, remember to choose wisely. Make sure you are speaking to someone in the area that you need counseling. Otherwise you could be led to things not in God's plan for your life.

DAY 58

✝

1 John 3:16-17 "This is how we've come to understand and experience love: Christ sacrificed his life for us. This is why we ought to live sacrificially for our fellow believers, and not just be out for ourselves. If you see some brother or sister in need and have the means to do something about it but turn a cold shoulder and do nothing, what happens to God's love? It disappears. And you made it disappear."

Today and every day, remember the ultimate sacrifice that Jesus had for us. He gave His life so we could live. His sacrifice teaches us about unconditional love. Showing that love to everyone including perfect strangers is a must. If we do not live with God at the forefront we are mocking him and discounting the love He has shown by sending His son and thus discounting the sacrifice Jesus gave for us to have it all. Your success or lack of is nothing without God's love. Embrace, share and be the love, because if you do not and the loves disappears you leave the door wide open for the enemy to come steal, kill, and destroy.

DAY 59

✟

Psalm 27:14 "Wait on the Lord; be of good courage, And He shall strengthen your heart; Wait, I say, on the Lord!"

Today, you have dreams and aspirations. God gave you a vision and He wants it to come into fruition. In order for that to happen, you must be patient. You must wait. One of the hardest things to do as believers and as individuals is to wait. We always want to rush God. We want instant success and instant gratification. We want to win the lottery. We want it all not now, but right now. God just wants us to wait. There is a reason as to why God has not brought you into what he has for you. Are you ready? Are you willing? Have you been putting God first? The answers are between you and God. The wait is not to punish you. It is to strengthen you. It is to increase your testimony. You must remember that every test and trial is not just to prepare you for what God is about to bring you into, but it is also to allow you to be a testimony that gets the next person to where God wants them to be.

DAY 60

☩

1 John 1:9 "If we confess our sin, He is faithful and just and will forgive us [of] our sins and to cleanse us from all unrighteousness."

Today you live each day with some form of sin in our lives. For most of us that sin is not something we seek out to have. It may be an untruth here and there. But no matter what it is sin. The truth is that God wants to forgive you. We are not perfect creations. The only pure perfection is God himself. He loves us so much that he simply wants us to ask him for forgiveness and he will forgive. Simply ask and you shall receive. Believe that today. God only wants the best for you. Sin, no matter what the sin is, can be forgiven if you just ask. As we grow each day we want to always put our best effort to be our best self and that includes asking for forgiveness and letting God cleanse of that impurity that plagues us most.

DAY 61

✟

2 Peter 3:18 "But grow in the grace and knowledge of our Lord and Savior Jesus Christ. To him be the glory both now and forever. Amen."

Today, take joy in God's word. Learn more of our Lord and Savior Jesus Christ. Understand that the grace of God is always with you, now and forever. Choose to focus on that today. No matter what may arise, focus on his grace.

DAY 62

✝

Leviticus 26: 3-4 "If you follow my decrees and are careful to obey my commands, I will send you rain in its season, and the ground will yield its crops and the trees their fruit."

Today, God wants you to put Him first in all that you do. He wants you to try your best to be like Christ. Be a true Christian. Obey the commandments. Failure to do so only knocks you further and further behind. If you learn to put God first in everything that you do, He will give you everything you want and need. God has called you to be the head and not the tail. He wants you to be successful. He wants you to be a light in a world that is otherwise dark. With that He wants to shower you with the riches of this land, spiritually and materially. So keep God first in everything that you do and you will get everything that you need and want.

DAY 63

✞

Ephesians 4:2 "Be completely humble and gentle; be patient, bearing with one another in love."

Today is a day to be humble. You must reverence in being one who has humility. As things come up today, approach it with patience. Approach it with love. Approach it with a mind to understand. When praised, be thankful not boastful. Being humble is what God wants. Pride has no room at the table.

DAY 64

✞

James 1:22 "Do not merely listen to the word, and so deceive yourselves. Do what it says."

Today is not the time to be someone that listens and does not act. You have been going to trainings, listening to and reading books, and reading the word of God. Then what do you do? You do nothing at all. You have two ears to hear, one mouth to speak, but you also have to legs, two arms and two hands. Let's put them to action.

DAY 65

✝

Genesis 3:4 "When the woman saw that the fruit of the tree was good for food and pleasing to the eye, and also desirable for gaining wisdom, she took some and ate it. She also gave some to her husband, who was with her, and he ate it."

Today, as you face what the day has to bring just remember that just because something looks good, sounds good and may give what you think you want, know it may not be what it seems. It may be the very thing that takes what is precious to you, away from you. Don't lose focus today. Don't get distracted.

DAY 66

✞

Ephesians 4:15 "but, speaking the truth in love, may grow up in all things into Him who is the head—Christ—"

Today, Christ wants you to be truthful in your ways. When interacting with the world remember that Christ is the head of your life. Do not conform to those things that are not of Him. Remember to speak the truth and speak the truth with love.

DAY 67

✝

Proverbs 4:14-17 "Do not set foot on the path of the wicked or walk in the way of evildoers. Avoid it, do not travel on it; turn from it and go on your way. For they cannot rest until they do evil; they are robbed of sleep till they make someone stumble. They eat the bread of wickedness and drink the wine of violence."

When you were a child you were taught right from wrong. Today, those same warnings are still present in your life. Everyone and everything is not for your good. Recognize it for what it is. There are people that are against you. Today, live and breathe anything that will keep you on the path of righteousness. Be aware, take notice and then move as far away as possible from those that will lead you off that path. Everything that God has for you is for you, but in order to get it, you must get rid of those things, those people, and even those factors that lead you to everything except what God has for you.

DAY 68

✝

*2 Chronicles 20:15 "Thus says the L*ORD *to you: 'Do not be afraid nor dismayed because of this great multitude, for the battle is not yours, but God's."*

Today, things may frustrate you. You may feel as you go through life, like you are losing more than winning. Remember God id fighting the war of life. He wins if you just turn it all over to Him. Do not be stressed. Do not be afraid. Do not have doubt. Do not live in negativity. Sit back, relax, let go, and let God.

DAY 69

✝

Proverbs 10:14 "Wise people store up knowledge, But the mouth of the foolish is near destruction."

Today is a day to remember that you are wise. As someone that is wise, you still must keep expanding your mind. Keep gaining knowledge that can push you to go beyond your limits and beyond your comfort zone. By keeping your mind strong you enable yourself to keep foolishness away from you. If you don't take in knowledge, then you will be left behind mentally. Lack of knowledge can destroy you. Sharpen your mind. Feed your mind and read.

DAY 70

✟

Ephesians 4:32 "And be kind to one another, tenderhearted, forgiving one another, even as God in Christ forgave you."

Today, regardless of what is coming at you, remember to extend a kind word to someone. Focus your energy on making someone else smile. God loves when you show love to one another. If you have a problem with someone, go to them and resolve it. Forgive and forget. Sometimes, that is the hardest thing for us to do. But when you forgive, Christ also forgives. In fact, Christ is quicker to forgive you then you are of others. Today, focus your efforts on being more like him. Live your days with love and forgiveness.

DAY 71

✝

Proverbs 16:11 "Sensible people control their temper; they earn respect by overlooking wrongs."

Today understand that it's to your best interest to control your temper. Do not rush to anger. Don't let the insensitivity of others drive you to uncontrollable actions. Don't let it drive you to say something you will regret. Remember to be smart about the situation. Smart people know how to hold their tongue. Smart people know how to think before reacting. More importantly they know how to forgive and forget. Look past the wrong that has been done against you. God will be pleased when you do. Remember that life is too short for you to have any regrets. Live on purpose, and with a purpose by putting God first and regrets will not be an issue.

DAY 72

✞

Proverbs 30:5-6 "Every word of God is pure; He is a shield to those who put their trust in Him. Do not add to His words, Lest He rebuke you and you be found and you a liar."

Today, God's word is true and pure. You should be true too. No one should wonder if you are being truthful every time you speak. No one should second guess your motives or your intentions. Do everything as unto the Lord and there will be no doubt.

DAY 73

✞

Proverbs 29:5 "A flattering neighbor is up to no good; he's probably planning to take advantage of you."

Today, be very careful of the things that are going on around you. Understand why they are happening. What may appear to be good may end up being not so good. Be sure the decisions you make are ones that help and not hinder. Watch the people around you too. Keep your eyes open. You do not want to be taken advantage of. Remember everything that is good is not necessarily good for you.

DAY 74

✝

Ecclesiastes 3:1 "There's an opportune time to do things, a right time for everything on the earth"

You have heard it more than once that there is a time and a place for everything. Today, you have to realize that now more than ever. Don't let obstacles draw you into a sense of being unsure. This is your time. This is what you have been waiting for. As the doors begin to open, run through them. Remember the promises that God has for you. He only wants the best for you. He wants to enlighten you and shine His glory upon you. Not now, but right now. It is up to you take ahold of all that He has for you and claim it as yours.

DAY 75

✝

Proverbs 28:2 "When the country is in chaos, everybody as a plan to fix it but it takes a leader of real understanding to straighten things out."

Today, you have been called to be a leader. Being a leader means more than standing for what it right. It is about showing others the way. God has put the light on you. He has designed you to be a leader that will leads lost souls out of darkness and into his glorious light. As a leader for Jesus Christ, you must put God first in everything that you do. Give him glory. Give Him honor and praise. Show others through your works that it is with God that you have what you have and are heading the right direction. Be the leader God has called you to be.

DAY 76

✝

Ecclesiastes 5:1 "Watch your step when you enter God's house. Enter to learn. That's far better than mindlessly offering a sacrifice, doing more harm than good."

Today, when you come to God asking for the things that you want, do not give false promises in return. You've seen it on television or even experienced it in your life. Someone is deathly ill, a child is missing or some other drastic thing is occurring and in the prayers to God, there is a bargain tied to it. I will do this, if God will do that. When you go to God with anything big or small, go with sincerity. Let God know that he is the light of your life. He is not asking for the formality of his Laws. He wants you to truly put him first. To love, honor and obey him. Go to God today with a sincere heart.

DAY 77

✝

Psalm 37:4 "Delight yourself also in the LORD, and He shall give you the desires of your heart."

Today, many times people go to God and say, "Your word says you will give me the desires of my heart and this is what I desire." They forget that the word also says "Delight yourself in the Lord, and He shall give you the desires of your heart." Jesus cannot be an afterthought in your mind and in your life. When you sit down today and evaluate all that you have vs all they you still want to accomplish, I want you to be honest with yourself as where exactly Jesus fits in. Does He really govern your life? Is He really in front of all that you do and hope to do? Many doors will remain closed to you until you fix where Jesus should be in every aspect of your life.

DAY 78

✝

Proverbs 1:7 "The fear of the LORD is the beginning of knowledge, But fools despise wisdom and instruction."

Today, having the fear of the Lord is a disposition that should resonate deep in your heart. Your fear of the Lord should lead you to gain knowledge, power, freedom and success, just to name a few, by holding such a disposition. A person with a heart full of foolishness does not want the added wisdom or the comfort that comes with it. They see it as a nuisance, especially since they believe they know it all and thus, have no fear.

DAY 79

✞

Psalm 39:7 "And now, Lord, what do I wait for? My hope is in You."

Today, this scripture is a rhetorical question for you. God has so many plans for you and He wants you to be righteous. He wants you to be right with Him. He doesn't want you to half-step, having one foot in the door and one foot out of the door. So the question is for you. What are you waiting for to make things right with the Lord? Your hope is in Him. Get to Him. Give to Him. Accept Him whole heartedly. In fact, why are you waiting to do those things that interest you most? In order to succeed in every area of your life, you have to accept Jesus Christ and put God first. Your hope for everything is in Him.

DAY 80

✝

Jeremiah 1:19 "They will fight against you but will not overcome you, for I am with you and will rescue you," declares the LORD"

Today, it may seem like every step that you take forward is one that is met with much resistance. I say to you now that all you need to do is turn to the Lord. He will rescue you from the uncertainty that you may be up against. The Lord is with you always. He understands everything even before it happens. Turn to Him now like you never have before.

DAY 81

✝

Isaiah 55: 8-9 "For My thoughts are not your thoughts, nor are your ways my ways," says the Lord. "For as the heavens are higher than the earth, so are my ways higher than your ways, and my thoughts than your thoughts.

Today, remember that God does not think the way you or I think. He certainly does not act the way you or I act. In fact, his thoughts and actions are so far from ours that in relation it is equivalent to how far the heavens are from the earth. Since there is such massive difference, you cannot expect God to move, act, react or do anything in the time frame that we as humans would. God is God. He is perfect. He will always be there for you and He will answer your prayers in the timeframe that He sees fit. Remember that when you are asking for things and upset when you don't have them immediately or in the time frame that you think you should have it.

DAY 82

✝

Psalm 40:2-3 "He also brought me up out of a horrible pit, Out of the miry clay, and set my feet upon a rock, and established my steps. He has put a new song in my mouth—Praise to our God; Many will see it and fear, and will trust in the LORD."

Today, whatever it is that you may be going through, know that God can bring you out. Sometimes you may feel like you can't get a good grip and everything is falling through your fingers. Nothing seems to be going right, or just when it should be going right, just like the snap of a finger, it turns and goes completely wrong. Don't be frustrated by these things. God has set you on solid ground. He has established a solid foundation for you. God has done and will continue to do all of these things and more if you just put your trust in Him.

DAY 83

✞

Isaiah 26:3 "He will keep in perfect peace all those who trust in him, whose thoughts turn often to the Lord!"

Today, no matter what the day brings, you will be in perfect peace. Just keep your thoughts on Him. If something unexpected comes your way, turn to the Lord. Good or bad, your thoughts should always turn to Him as He is the one that lights your path and guides you through each day.

DAY 84

✝

Proverbs 3:5-6 "Trust in the LORD with all your heart, and lean not on your own understanding; in all your ways acknowledge Him, And He shall direct your paths."

Today, the Lord is here to lead you and guide you through each and every day. Often times, instead of turning to the Lord, we turn to others including ourselves and then wonder why things are not going the way that they should. Do not let those things that are not of Him keep you from Him. He is something and someone that you should carry with you daily.

DAY 85

✝

Psalm 119:105 "Your word is a lamp to my feet and a light to my path."

Today, follow the light. God's word is the light that helps lead you in the right direction. Ensure that your mind is fed with his word each and every day. It will sustain you when times are hard and rough. It will reassure you in times of uncertainty. It will comfort you in times of loss. It will love you when it seems no love is present. God's word will do all this and more for you.

DAY 86

✝

Psalm 139:23-24 "Search me, God, and know my heart; test me and know my anxious thoughts. See if there is any offensive way in me, and lead me in the way everlasting."

Today ask God to help you get rid of anything that is not of him. He will do that if you only ask. But as He begins to remove things not just from you but your life you have to recognize that it is a move that must take place in order for you to fulfill your purpose in Christ Jesus.

DAY 87

✝

Psalm 55:22 "Cast your cares on the LORD AND he will sustain you; he will never let the righteous be shaken."

Today, all you have to do is turn it over to the Lord. You feel it coming. Don't be anxious, don't be afraid. Just let go and let God. He will sustain you. He will ensure that you are strong and mighty. He will keep you through it all. Relax and release it to the Lord. Not some of it, all of it. God already knows what you need, He is just waiting on you to get out of the way and let Him have his way.

DAY 88

✝

Proverbs 31:10 "Who can find a virtuous woman? For her price [is] far above rubies"

Today, a virtuous woman is a woman with high standards of moral and respect in every area of her life. She is hard to find, but she is out there. Men, if you are looking for a virtuous woman, know that her worth cannot be measured. Know that once you find her, you have to treat her as the valuable jewel that she is. Women, if you want to be a virtuous woman, you have to be able to set yourself apart from everyone else. When someone sees you, speaks with you, enjoys your company, they will automatically know that you are "different". You are not "typical". If both men and women keep God first in their lives, God will ensure she is what man is looking for and man will treat her as the priceless jewel she is. Side note for a woman: it is not for you to tell a man that you are virtuous it is for him to find out if you are virtuous. Actions speak louder than words.

DAY 89

✝

Romans 1:16 "For I am not ashamed of the gospel, because it is the power of God that brings salvation to everyone who believes: first to the Jew, then to the Gentile."

Today, God is not anything to be ashamed of and neither is his word. His word is here to bring salvation to everyone. Spread the word. Share it with a friend or a co-worker. Share it with someone you just met. His word will not only lead people to salvation, it will also help those that need help. It will be that tool, that piece of something that they have been waiting for that gets them from point A to point B.

DAY 90

✝

John 14:27 "Peace I leave with you; my peace I give you. I do not give to you as the world gives. Do not let your hearts be troubled and do not be afraid." Today God's peace is with you always.

Do not be afraid that you are alone in the troubles that you have. Remember, God is with you always. He will give a peace that will comfort you and leave you in a place of rest. He will leave you with a feeling like a weight has been lifted off of you. Just give it all to God and feel his peace. Welcome his peace.

DAY 91

✝

Proverbs 31: 29 "Many daughters have done virtuously, but thou [excels] them all."

Today, live with excellence and virtue. Just like in this scripture, you want to be the one that they say is better than the rest. You want to be the one that breeds success in everyone's life starting with your own. You want to be the one that others will look up to with respect and want to be like. You want to excel them all.

DAY 92

✝

John 15:13 "Greater love has no one than this: to lay down one's life for one's friends.

Today, love like you have never loved before. Love everyone like you would give your life for them. This is the kind of love that Jesus has for you. He gave his life for you. There is no greater love than the sacrificial love of the Lord. Share that love with others.

DAY 93

†

Romans 8:28 "And we know that in all things God works for the good of those who love him, who have been called according to his purpose."

Today, know that whatever happens, it is all God's will. All things work for his will and to your good. Even the bad things draw you closer to Him. Don't get upset if something does not go your way today. Understand that everything does happen for a reason. God has a plan and purpose for you. The good, the bad, and the ugly help line things up for your purpose.

DAY 94

✟

Romans 12:10-13 *"Be devoted to one another in love. Honor one another above yourselves. Never be lacking in zeal, but keep your spiritual fervor, serving the Lord. Be joyful in hope, patient in affliction, [and] faithful in prayer. Share with the Lord's people who are in need. Practice hospitality."*

Today, live each day putting others before you. Do not put them before God, but do love them, encourage them, respect them, be kind to them, and treat them the way you would want to be treated. Be patient and prayerful and share the goodness of the Lord with them. Doing these things is pleasing to the Lord.

DAY 95

✝

John 14:16-17 "And I will pray the Father, and He will give you another Helper, that He may abide with you forever the Spirit of truth, whom the world cannot receive, because it neither sees Him nor knows Him; but you know Him, for He dwells with you and will be in you."

Today, the Holy Spirit is with you and dwells with you always. Jesus promised before his crucifixion to leave you a helper. Jesus leaves you the Holy Spirit. Know that as you live each day and as obstacles come up, you have the Holy Spirit. The Holy Spirit is a comforter in your time of need.

DAY 96

✝

Proverbs 31:20 "Charm is deceptive, and beauty is fleeting; but a woman [man] who fears the LORD is to be praised."

Today, it is one thing to have charm and good looks, but you must have more. God is looking for someone who also has the fear of the Lord in their heart, because that person deserves praise. A God-fearing person knows the order that God has established. Remember this when you chose your mate. Look at the mate that you have and see if the fear of the Lord is there. Someone who fears God will treat you the way you should be treated, because God would not have it any other way.

DAY 97

✞

2 Corinthians 5:17 "Therefore, if anyone is in Christ, the new creation has come: The old has gone, the new is here!"

Today, and every single day, know that you are renewed in Christ Jesus. When you accept Him as your Lord and savior, He washes away all your past. He forgets what you were and begins to mold you into what you should be which is a guiding light to others, leading them to Him. Understand that when you accepted Jesus into your heart, He saved you. He saved you from your past. He saved you from everything that you were. But He also forgave you and renewed you. Now you must now forgive yourself. Leave the past in the past. Live each day as if it is the first day of the rest of your life with Jesus by your side.

DAY 98

✝

Ephesians 2:8 "For it is by grace you have been saved, through faith—and this is not from yourselves, it is the gift of God"

Today God has given you a gift. You accepted that gift when you accepted Jesus into your heart as your Lord and savior. Therefore it is his by his grace and your faith that you are saved. Now take this gift, go out into the world and share the gift. Let other now of the goodness of Jesus Christ and what God has done and is doing for you.

DAY 99

✟

Ephesians 2:10 "For we are God's handiwork, created in Christ Jesus to do good works, which God prepared in advance for us to do."

Today God has made you what you are, beautiful in your own right. You were created to do the work of the Lord long before God knew you. Live out your purpose with his good will in mind. He has already given you everything you need to achieve every goal you have.

DAY 100

✝

1 Corinthians 6:19 "Do you not know that your bodies are temples of the Holy Spirit, who is in you, whom you have received from God? You are not your own;"

Today, know that your body is a temple. The Holy Spirit lives in you. Treat your body like it is precious gem worthy of no less than the best. Eat right, drink right, nourish right, and love right. Show God that you can take care of the precious gift He has given to you, your body.

DAY 101

✞

Philippians 4:8 "Finally, brothers and sisters, whatever is true, whatever is noble, whatever is right, whatever is pure, whatever is lovely, whatever is admirable—if anything is excellent or praiseworthy—think about such things."

Today, focus your thoughts on positive things. Get rid of the negativity. When negativity comes your way, ignore it. You have better things to do with your time than acknowledge anything that is not of the Lord. Negative is not of the Lord. Do not waste your time entertaining it or anyone that brings it your way.

DAY 102

✞

Deuteronomy 8:18 "But remember the L__ORD__ your God, for it is he who gives you the ability to produce wealth, and so confirms his covenant, which he swore to your ancestors, as it is today."

Today, God is the reason you have what you have. He has blessed you with the talent and the knowledge to do anything you want to do. You are destined for greatness. You are destined to succeed. The blessings that God has for you are for you. Don't waste it. Go after it and get it done!

DAY 103

✞

Ephesians 3:20 "Now to Him who is able to do exceedingly abundantly above all that we ask or think, according to the power that works in us,"

Today, God can do anything that you ask and more. You have to know that. God is your provider. He is your helper. He is your confidant. He is your joy. He is your hope for tomorrow. He will do above and beyond what you ask or think. But you have to believe it. The power of your belief will fulfill your hopes and dreams through Jesus Christ. What do you believe Him for today?

DAY 104

✝

Mark. 11:24 "Therefore I tell you, whatever you ask for in prayer, believe that you have received it, and it will be yours."

Today, I want you to check your belief system. Do you really believe that you can have everything that you want? I'm here to let you know that you can. You just have to believe it. Ask and you shall receive, but you have to also believe that you will receive it.

DAY 105

✟

Mark. 11:25-26 "And when you stand praying, if you hold anything against anyone, forgive them, so that your Father in heaven may forgive you your sins"

Today, when you go to God in prayer, you cannot ask for forgiveness if you are not willing to forgive others as well. What most people fail to realize is that with forgiveness you must also forget. That means you have to let it go. Let it go because when God forgives you, He lets it go. He doesn't hold onto it and bring it up to you the next time you disappoint Him. So do the same for others. Forgive, forget, and then let it go.

DAY 106

✝

3 John 1:2 "Dear friend, I pray that you may enjoy good health and that all may go well with you, even as your soul is getting along well."

Today, God only wants the best for us. We are his children no less. He wants the best for our entire being, including mind, body, and spirit. He wants us to enjoy good health for our physical self even if our spiritual self is getting along just fine. Take time to take care of yourself. Our lives are full of being "busy". Don't be too busy to take some time for you. You will not regret making sure you are the best that you can be.

DAY 107

✝

Proverbs 4:23 "Keep your heart with all diligence, for out of it spring the issues of life."

Today, watch your heart. Guard it with all necessity. Life and everything from it begins with the heart. We are emotional creatures. Emotion starts with your heart. Do not let anyone have your heart that is not worthy of having it. Be sure that the person you give your heart to will take care of it as you would theirs.

DAY 108

✝

2 Timothy 1:7 "For God has not given us a spirit of fear, but of power and of love and of a sound mind."

Today, don't let uncertainty let fear into your life. I know the fear that you may feel sometimes. Maybe you are one that is afraid of speaking in front of large crowds or you have a fear of rejection. Whatever the fear, God wants you to know that you have the power and love of a sound mind.

DAY 109

✟

Matthew 17:20 "He replied, "Because you have so little faith. Truly I tell you, if you have faith as small as a mustard seed, you can say to this mountain, 'Move from here to there,' and it will move. Nothing will be impossible for you."

Today, you have got to believe in what God can do for you. Most of your problems come because you do not truly have faith in God's ability to take care of your situation. I promise you, that if you just turn it over to the Lord He will work it out. Now you have to believe it too. This scripture says it best. A mustard seed is so small, extremely small in fact. All you need is faith that is the size of a mustard seed. The possibilities are endless.

DAY 110

✞

James 4:3 "When you ask, you do not receive, because you ask with wrong motives, that you may spend what you get on your pleasures."

Today, when you go to God, are you going to Him with the right intentions? Are you going to Him with your heart in the right place? Everyone wants to be rich and wealthy, but God does not allow everyone to achieve great wealth. Make sure your heart and your intentions are in the right place in everything that you do, especially when you go to God.

DAY 111

✞

Deuteronomy 28:1 "If you fully obey the LORD your God and carefully follow all his commands I give you today, the LORD your God will set you high above all the nations on earth."

Today, you will receive blessings for obedience, there is nothing like it. God promises you the world if you simply follow all of his commandments. Don't think too much about it. Just do it. Listen to his word and follow his word.

DAY 112

✝

Proverbs 3:9-10 "Honor the Lord by giving him the first part of all your income and he will fill your barns with wheat and barley and overflow your wine vats with the finest wines."

Today, you work and push hard at your jobs and your businesses, which are blessings from the Lord. It is blessings from God that you have them at all. You must honor Him with the first part of your income in every aspect of your life. All increase that you obtain, you must put the first portion back to the Lord in order for Him to continue to keep blessing you. If you give of your first income you will receive an over flow of blessings and want for nothing.

DAY 113

✝

Philemon 1:6 "And I pray that as you share your faith with others it will grip their lives too, as they see the wealth of good things in you that come from Christ Jesus."

Today, I encourage you to share your faith with others. You never know what people are going through on any given day. Sharing your faith can give them a breakthrough. It also restores their faith and more importantly lead them to Christ. Believe it or not, people are watching you. When you share the good things that come from having a relationship with Jesus Christ, you also inspire others to do the same.

DAY 114

✝

John 14:13-14 "And I will do whatever you ask in my name, so that the Father may be glorified in the Son. You may ask me for anything in my name, and I will do it."

Today, God wants you to know that whatever it is that you need, all you have to do is just ask in His name and He will do it. Glorify Him in the good and in the bad. You can ask Him for anything and He will do it.

DAY 115

✝

*Proverbs 10:22 "The blessing of the L*ORD *makes one rich, and He adds no sorrow with it."*

Today, do not be sad when God blesses you. His blessings make you rich in all ways not just financially. He enriches you with knowledge and expertise to share. He enriches you with energy to do more. He enriches you with experience to pass. He enriches you with his light to pull others out of darkness. What He does not do is make your life rich for you to be unhappy.

DAY 116

✝

Philippians 3:13 *"Brethren, I do not count myself to have apprehended; but one thing I do, forgetting those things which are behind and reaching forward to those things which are ahead."*

Today, forget those things of that past that seem to be hindering your from moving forward. The past is just that, the past. Every day that you wake up you have been leaving whatever happened the day before in the past. Reach forward to the things that make life worth living. You have a vision in you. You have dreams in you. You have to go after them. Make your dreams a reality. One of my mentors lives by the motto "Live Your Dreams…It's Possible." And it is possible. Remember Jesus lives in you. With Jesus you can accomplish anything.

DAY 117

✞

Psalm 6:8 "Go, leave me now, you men of evil deeds, for the Lord has heard my weeping."

Today, you may be experiencing some challenges. Do not cry and be sad for too long. You have to praise God through your circumstance. Prior to that you, you have to rid yourself of anyone that is not of Him. If they are not lifting you up, then they are tearing you down. Stop letting others tear you down when God is lifting you. Praise Him through your circumstance. Praise Him for what he is about to bring you into. He has heard your prayers and has seen your tears. He is working it out for you.

DAY 118

✟

Proverbs 25:11 "The right word at the right time is like a custom-made piece of jewelry, and a wise friend's timely reprimand is like a gold ring slipped on your finger."

Today, kindness in your words can go so far. The truth of your words can go farther. Respect your friends by telling the truth. Accept when someone tells you the truth. No one likes to be lied to. Kindness shown in words is reflective of the love of the Lord.

DAY 119

✝

Psalm 100:1-4 "Make a joyful noise unto the LORD, all ye lands. Serve the LORD with gladness: come before his presence with singing. Know ye that the LORD he is God: it is he that hath made us, and not we ourselves; we are his people, and the sheep of his pasture. Enter into his gates with thanksgiving, and into his courts with praise: be thankful unto him, and bless his name."

Today, give thanks and sing praises from within because you have been given another day. God created you and He woke you up this morning. You have so much to be thankful for. Think of your situation, whatever is bothering you most. Now keep this in mind the next time you want to beat yourself up or the next time you think things cannot get any worse. There is someone somewhere out there in the world that has it much worse than you. Someone didn't wake up this morning. That someone could have been you. Thank God now for another day.

DAY 120

✝

Psalm 19:14 "Let the words of my mouth and the meditation of my heart be acceptable in your sight, O LORD, my strength and my Redeemer"

Today, begin the day by keeping a clear head. Make sure the words that come out of your mouth reflect the Lord. The Lord is your strength and He is your redeemer. He is the light that leads others from darkness. Share that light with others today. Be the force of reason not the wrath of unrighteousness.

DAY 121

✝

Psalm 67:1-4 "God be merciful to us and bless us, and cause His face to shine upon us, that your way may be known on earth, your salvation among all nations. Let the people praise You, O God; Let all the people praise you. Oh, let the nations be glad and sing for joy! For you shall judge the people righteously, and govern the nations on earth."

Today, God has been merciful to you. He has blessed you. He has shined is face on you. He did this for your salvation. Share that salvation with others. Spread the gospel of Jesus to anyone and everyone. Every day that God wakes you up, He gives you another opportunity to get it done. He has given you another opportunity to make today better than yesterday. Take the gift of life and live it to the fullest. More importantly live life with a purpose and on purpose. You only have one life to live.

DAY 122

✝

Proverbs 15:15 "When a man is gloomy, everything seems to go wrong; when he is cheerful, everything seems right!"

Today, you must start with a smile. It will take you so much further than a frown. Get your mind right. Play some loud music or read an inspirational book. Either way you must do something you love. Something that will have a smile on your face no matter what you encounter. If your mind is happy, your actions will follow. Your body follows your mind.

DAY 123

✟

2 Corinthians 4:16 "That is why we never give up. Though our bodies are dying, our inner strength in the Lord is growing every day"

Today, and every day, you are given a chance to grow. Some grow more than others. We grow spiritually. We grow financially. We grow emphatically. More importantly we should be growing in the Lord. As each day passes, we also grow older. While our physical body grows older, our inner self should be growing with the life of the Lord.

DAY 124

✝

Proverbs 27:5-6 "Open rebuke is better than hidden love! Wounds from a friend are better than kisses from an enemy!"

Today, true friends mean well, even when they hurt you. What you have to watch out for is that person that pretends to be here for you. Watch out for the person that will smile in your face, but secretly wants to take your place. They focus on being just like the number two version of you versus the number one version of themselves. Even when a friend treats you bad, you get over it, and get on with your day. Your enemy coming for you, that's a different story. Keep your eyes open.

DAY 125

✝

Proverbs 15:28 "A good man thinks before he speaks; the evil man pours out his evil words without a thought."

Today, whatever is in your heart will also come out of your mouth. A righteous man speaks words knowledge and his words are right. Evil people could care less about the words that are coming out of their mouths. They are foolish and cause nothing but trouble. Be one that is wise and prove your wisdom with the words that come out of your mouth. Speak truth today. Speak life today. Speak words with the love of the Lord. Control yourself always and control your mouth too.

DAY 126

✝

Proverbs 15:17 "It is better to eat soup with someone you love than steak with someone you hate."

Today, please remember that just because you can have a good meal, eating with someone you hate or despise is worse than eating modestly with someone you love. Choose the people that you spend your time with wisely. If they don't deserve your time, then they are only wasting your time. You do not have time to waste. There is too much that needs to be done for the Kingdom of God. There is just as much that needs to be done to get you to your purpose.

DAY 127

✟

Proverbs 12:9 "It is better to get your hands dirty—and eat, than to be too proud to work—and starve."

Today, we live in a society where things are praised and people are praised rather than God. Hard work is no longer the way to the top. The media exacerbates everything and down-plays God and anything that remotely leans towards religion. Be different. Be righteous. Putting on a flashy image while you starve gets you nowhere and leaves you hungry. Some people try to make themselves out to be more and have more than what is actually so. To that, I say be real. Be honest and be open.

DAY 128

✝

Proverbs 12:18 "Some people like to make cutting remarks, but the words of the wise soothe and heal."

Today, be kind with your words. Nothing can cut a person deeper than sharp words pushed hard at them. Be better than that. Be the person that uplifts someone not the person that tears someone down.

DAY 129

✞

Psalm 27:1 "The Lord is my light and my salvation, whom shall I fear? The Lord is the stronghold of my life, of whom shall I be afraid."

Today, there is nothing to fear. You are a child of God, made in his image. He loves you and knew you before you were born. He sent his son Jesus as your salvation. Since Jesus is your light and your salvation, why would you entertain fear? What would you be afraid of?

DAY 130

✝

Proverbs 15:3 "The Lord is watching everywhere and keeps his eye on both the evil and the good."

Today, understand that no matter what is going on, God knows it. He sees all and hears all. Nothing gets past God, neither the good nor the bad. He knows what you are doing as well as what everyone else is doing. And for those that are doing good deeds, He is smiling on you.

DAY 131

✝

Proverbs 1:33 "But whoever listens to me will live in safety and be at ease, without fear of harm."

Today, it does not matter what happens, you will be safe with God's protection. Live each day in the security of the Lord. He shields you from uncertainty. He keeps you out of harm's way. Stay focused on that each and every day.

DAY 132

✝

Proverbs 15:31-32 "If you profit from constructive criticism, you will be elected to the wise men's hall of fame. But to reject criticism is to harm yourself and your own best interests."

Today, seek out criticism and use it to grow. Success will never happen for you if you cannot take criticism and make the changes necessary to move forward.

DAY 133

✝

1 Peter 5:5 "In the same way, you who are younger, submit yourselves to your elders. All of you clothe yourselves with humility toward one another, because, "God opposes the proud but shows favor to the humble."

Today, we have always been taught to respect our elders. But we must also respect each other and have some humility. Pride will get you nowhere. God shows favor to those that let pride go. So remember to humble yourself with each other.

DAY 134

✝

Proverbs 12:19 "Truth stands the test of time; lies are soon exposed."

Today, you want to be a person that is looked upon as an honest person, a person that always tells the truth. Lies get you nowhere. It's too much extra info to keep up with. Besides, at the end of the day, what is done in the dark will come to light, and your lies will be front and center.

DAY 135

✝

Proverbs 12:22 "God delights in those who keep their promises and abhors those who don't."

Today, be a person of your word. Even the smallest of promises kept is smiled on by God. If you go ahead making promises that you cannot keep, you bring sadness to God. Be the person He can be proud of. He loves you and only wants the best for you and the best of you. Say what you mean and mean what you say.

DAY 136

✝

1 Peter 2:17 "Honor all people. Love the brotherhood. Fear God. Honor the king."

Today is a new day. Remember what God says to honor all people. Love everyone with the Love of the Lord. Doing these things is pleasing to God. Fear God with the love of knowing that He is the Kings of Kings and Lord of Lords.

DAY 137

✝

Proverbs 12:25 "Anxious hearts are very heavy, but a word of encouragement does wonders!"

Today, someone may be going through a difficult time. Be kind to them. Give them some words of encouragement. Life gives each of us up and downs. It throws us curve balls and makes us questions everything that we know. Sometimes, the kind words of a friend will help relieve any added stress.

DAY 138

✝

Exodus 14:14 "The LORD will fight for you; you need only to be still."

Today, when the enemy comes against you, just turn it over to the Lord. He will always fight your battles. There is no need to try to do it all by yourself. That is why we have the Lord.

DAY 139

✝

Psalm 45:1 "God is our refuge and strength, an ever-present help in trouble."

Today, expect the unexpected. Good or bad, God is with us, shielding us and giving us strength. He is our help in time of trouble. The trouble can be physical, spiritual, or mental. God will never fail you. He will see you through. Know when the enemy starts to trip you up today, God is with you. When traffic begins to get heavy, God is with you. When news of a loved one's unfortunate situation reaches you, God is when you. When it begins to rain in your life metaphorically or actually, God is with you. He is a present help. Meaning not a now help but a right now help. God is with you, giving you strength.

DAY 140

✝

Exodus 20:20 "Moses said to the people, "Do not be afraid. God has come to test you, so that the fear of God will be with you to keep you from sinning."

Today, you may be tested. But just like Moses said to the people, "God will be with you to keep you from sinning." So let the test come. You are not to be afraid. You will overcome!

DAY 141

✝

Exodus 14:13 "Do not be afraid. Stand firm and you will see the deliverance the LORD will bring you today. The Egyptians you see today you will never see again."

Today, your enemies will be moved out of your presence. The Lord will bring you out of any misery. He fights all that is against you. So stand firm today. Be unmovable today. Let the Lord handle all of it for you. There is no need to be afraid of what is to come because the Lord will see you through. No matter what comes your way, remember that the Lord will see you through.

DAY 142

✝

Proverbs 19:21 "Many plans are in a man's mind, but it is the Lord's purpose for him that will stand."

Today, God has a purpose and a plan for your life. Man can make many plans for you, but only God's plan will stand. Be sure to follow God's plan as His plan will prevail over man's plan.

DAY 143

✝

Psalm 56:3 "When I am afraid, I put my trust in you."

Today, instead of being afraid of the uncertainty or afraid of what is to come, put your trust in God. He is here for you always. He will not fail you. Just put your trust in Him and watch what He will do.

DAY 144

✝

Philippians 4:4 "Rejoice in the Lord always. I will say it again: Rejoice!"

Today, praise God for all that He has done and all that He is about to do. Don't let uncertainty keep you from everything God has for you. Rejoice now. Rejoice always. Give thanks to the Lord for He is good. Let your praise be continuous today.

DAY 145

✟

Colossians 3:2 "Set your minds on things above, not on earthly things."

Today, as each day goes by, know that your vision, your ambition and your endeavors will increase. Don't let those things that are not of God keep you from God. Your mind and your actions should always keep Him first. Keeping His will is what you should do. As a result, He will keep giving you the vision, the ambition and the desire to accomplish those endeavors that matter to you most.

DAY 146

✝

John 6:38 "For I have come down from heaven not to do my own will and purpose but to do the will and purpose of Him Who sent me."

Just like Jesus was sent for a purpose, you too have a purpose. Whatever your purpose is, know that it is God's will. Find your purpose, and then tap into your purpose. Know what your purpose is and do it with excellence. Remember God knew you before you were born and, therefore, already knows your purpose.

DAY 147

✝

Psalm 145:9 "The LORD is good to all."

Today is a beautiful day. God woke you up this morning. The Lord is good. He is good to all. Today, take a lesson from Him. Watch your tongue. Watch your attitude. Greet people with a smile and not a frown. Show the love of the Lord through you. Show how good the Lord is through you.

DAY 148

✝

Psalm 121:1-2 "I lift up my eyes to the mountains—where does my help come from? My help comes from the LORD, the Maker of heaven and earth."

Today, you may find yourself turning to various people and things to bring about an answer to your questions. You may even be turning to these people for help with minor and major things. There is no need to turn to anyone but the Lord. For the Lord is where your help comes from.

DAY 149

✞

Romans 15:13 "May the God of hope fill you with all joy and peace as you trust in him, so that you may overflow with hope by the power of the Holy Spirit."

Today, I urge you to put your trust in God and, in return, receive the joy and peace to put your mind at ease. No need turning to anyone else. The power of the Holy Spirit and of God is with you always.

DAY 150

✝

Romans 8:38-39 "For I am convinced that neither death nor life, neither angels nor demons, neither the present nor the future, nor any powers, neither height nor depth, nor anything else in all creation, will be able to separate us from the love of God that is in Christ Jesus our Lord."

Today, God's love is so great that He gave us his son Jesus Christ. There is nothing in this world that can separate us from that love. That love is eternal. That love is the one thing that will always be with you.

DAY 151

✝

Psalm 121:8 "The LORD will watch over your coming and going both now and forevermore."

Today, the Lord sits high and low and sees all of the places you are coming from and going to. You cannot hide anything from the Lord. He is watching over you and will continue to watch over you.

DAY 152

✝

Psalm 150:6 "Let everything that has breath praise the Lord."

Today, God woke you up. He has allowed you to see another day. He has given you another chance to make today better than yesterday. Give praise to the Lord for the chance to make today your best day yet.

DAY 153

✝

2 Peter 3:9 "The Lord is not slow in keeping His promise, as some understand slowness. He is patient with you, not wanting anyone to perish, but everyone to come to repentance."

Today, just because something that you have asked God for does not happen as quickly as you would like, doesn't mean that He is slow moving. He know what you have, He knows what you need. All He wants from you is for you to keep Him first and know that He is God and He will provide all in due time.

DAY 154

✝

Proverbs 1:22 "How long will you simple ones love your simple ways? How long will mockers delight in mockery and fools hate knowledge?

Today, reach for greater knowledge than what you have. Stretch yourself to further today and every day. Don't settle for mediocre. Always strive for better, for greater, for more and it starts with knowledge. Knowledge is the key to unlocking every door that can give you everything. Expand your mind, and you will automatically expand your life.

DAY 155

✝

Isaiah 40:28 "Don't you yet understand? Don't you know by now that the everlasting God, the Creator of the farthest parts of the earth, never grows faint or weary? No one can fathom the depths of his understanding."

Today, it doesn't matter what you bring to God. He knows what you are going through. He understands and He has a plan. Bring all of your thoughts, your prayers, your cares and your concerns to God. He can handle it.

DAY 156

✝

Luke 6:31 "Do unto others as you would have them do unto you."

Today, treat people the way you want to be treated. It will get you where you ultimately want to go. Stepping on people and using people will get you small rewards that will crumble fast. You must be a genuine person. You must treat people right even if they do not treat you right. You will get exactly what you give out. Call it Karma if you want, but God says you will reap exactly what you sow.

DAY 157

✟

Matthew 28:29 "I am with you always."

Today, God is with you now and forever. Even when things are going good and when things are going not so good. He is here to guide you and keep you from hurt, harm and danger. He is here to show you the good inside of you and the good in others. He is here to share his son Jesus Christ with you. He is here to give you the life that you deserve. He is here with you always.

DAY 158

✞

Philippians 4:13 "I can do all things through Christ who strengthens me."

Today, know that you can do all things. Nothing can stop you. You have the power because you have Jesus Christ living in you. Don't doubt or let fear creep into your mind. Keep negativity away from you. With Jesus, you are content in everything and in every circumstance because He gives you strength. You can do all things that God is leading you to do.

DAY 159

✝

Psalm 136:1 "Give thanks to the Lord, for he is good. His love endures forever."

Today, sing it, shout it or say it: "Thanks to the Lord" because He is good. His love will endure and last forever. Give Him thanks today and always.

DAY 160

✝

2 Corinthians 12:9 "But he said to me, 'My grace is sufficient for you, for my power is made perfect in weakness.' Therefore I will boast all the more gladly about my weaknesses, so that Christ's power may rest on me."

Today, you are no longer weak because God's grace has given you power. Talk about your weaknesses so you may overcome them in Christ's power.

DAY 161

✟

2 Corinthians 4:18 "So we fix our eyes not on what is seen, but on what is unseen. For what is seen is temporary, but what is unseen is eternal."

Today, set your eyes on what you cannot see in front of you. That is your eternal home. This that you see is temporary. Focus on living with Jesus forever. The eternal life with God is the life you should always seek after.

DAY 162

✝

Galatians 2:20 "I have been crucified with Christ and I no longer live, but Christ lives in me. The life I live in the body, I live by faith in the Son of God, who loved me and gave himself for me."

Today, you live only because Christ lives in you. You have completely surrendered to God through Christ. Selfishness is no longer present. Greed is no longer present. Desires that lead you to focus only on you, no longer exist. Claim that today for yourself.

DAY 163

✟

1 John 3:23 "Love one another."

Today, I want you to love, yes L-O-V-E. This is simple and not hard to do because you have the love of God in you. So love one another today and always.

DAY 164

✝

1 John 4:7-8 "Dear friends, let us love one another, for love comes from God. Everyone who loves has been born of God and knows God. Whoever does not love does not know God, because God is love."

Today, love one another because you are born of God and God is love. Therefore, He who does not have the love of God does not know Him. You know you have God's love and you know that you love Him. Show that today.

DAY 165

✝

1 Corinthians 15:58 "Therefore, my dear brothers, stand firm. Let nothing move you. Always give yourselves fully to the work of the Lord, because you know that your labor in the Lord is not in vain."

Today, the work you are doing for the Lord is not in vain. Stand and do not move. Stand like the tree that has deep roots, unmovable. Let God be your light.

DAY 166

✞

Galatians 5:22-23 "But the fruit of the Spirit is love, joy, peace, patience, kindness, goodness, faithfulness, gentleness and self-control. Against such things there is no law."

Today, and every day, you must have and keep the fruit of the Spirit to guide you. Think of yourself as a bowl that holds the different fruits. There are apples, oranges, bananas, grapes, tangerines and others. These fruits are love, joy, peace, patience, kindness, goodness, faithfulness, gentleness and self-control.

DAY 167

✝

1 Thessalonians 5:18 "Give thanks in all circumstances for this is God's will for you in Christ Jesus."

Today, give thanks to God for everything no matter what. Good or bad, thank God today. Thank Him every day. If this day is not going as great as it should, thank Him. When you feel there is no way out, you must thank Him. When the day is the best day of your life, you must thank Him. More importantly, when the day comes and it seems that it is the worst day of your life, you must thank Him for what you are going through.

DAY 168

✝

1 Corinthians 10:13 "No temptation has seized you except what is common to man. And God is faithful; he will not let you be tempted beyond what you can bear. But when you are tempted, he will also provide a way out, so that you can stand up under it."

Today, you can withstand all that may come against you because He will provide a way for you to stand, to bear, or a way out. God is faithful. He will not leave you.

DAY 169

✞

Ephesians 6:12 "For we wrestle not against flesh and blood, but against principalities, against powers, against the rulers of the darkness of this world, against spiritual wickedness in high places."

Today, you don't have to fight physical people, principalities, powers or dark and wicked rulers because it is done spiritually. There is no need to be upset with what is happening in this world.

DAY 170

✝

Psalm 119:11 "I have hidden your word in my heart that I might not sin against you."

Today, you have God's word in your heart and that keeps you from sinning against Him. Focus on what is right. Run from what is wrong. Use His word to guide and keep you.

DAY 171

✝

Micah 6:8 "He has showed you, O man, what is good. And what does the Lord require of you? To act justly and to love mercy and to walk humbly with your God."

God has shown you the way you should act. He has shown you the way to love and to have mercy. Just walk humbly with God and take in all he has to offer.

DAY 172

✟

Romans 12:1 "Therefore, I urge you, brothers, in view of God's mercy, to offer your bodies as living sacrifices, holy and pleasing to God—this is your spiritual act of worship."

Today, when you worship God, make your whole body a sacrifice unto Him. Your mind, body and your soul all belong to Him. This is how you must worship Him.

DAY 173

✝

Proverbs 16:24 "Pleasant words are a honeycomb, sweet to the soul and healing to the bones."

Today let kind words come out of your mouth. Talk to people that way you want to be talked to. Have some respect and decency with you speak today. You will always go further in life with kind words. It does wonders for someone who really needs to hear good things.

DAY 174

✝

Acts 18:9 "One night the Lord spoke to Paul in a vision: 'Do not be afraid; keep on speaking, do not be silent."

Today, you can speak boldly as Paul did and not be afraid. God wants you to speak of His goodness. There is no need to be afraid. Speak with confidence knowing that God is with you.

DAY 175

✝

Romans 3:23 "For all have sinned and fall short of the glory of God"

Today, know that it is your sins that will keep you from God. Live each day striving to have no sin. Although there is no one without sin, we must do our very best to attempt to be without sin. When we do sin, ask for forgiveness and turn away from that sin, striving to not commit the same sin again.

DAY 176

✝

Luke 16:13 "No servant can serve two masters. Either he will hate the one and love the other, or he will be devoted to the one and despise the other. You cannot serve both God and Money."

Today, love God and serve Him and He will be everything to you and everything for you. Money will not give you everything. Certainly, it will secure you with the thought that there are now no problems because you have money. However, the more money that comes your way, the more problems that will come your way. With that said, look at it this way, where does God fit in if the most important thing to you is money? God does not compete with things of the world. So choose whom you will have. God can give you money, but money cannot give you God.

DAY 177

✝

Hebrews 11:1 "Now faith is the substance of things hoped for, the evidence of things not seen."

Today, when you hope for something and can't see a way that it could happen or come through, that is where your faith will make it. Faith takes you where your eyes cannot. Faith takes you beyond your vision. You must have faith today and always.

DAY 178

✞

Romans 10:9 "That if you confess with your mouth, "Jesus is Lord," and believe in your heart that God raised him from the dead you will be saved."

Today, you can be free with these words "Jesus is Lord," and believe in your heart that God did raise Jesus from the dead. You can and will be saved.

DAY 179

✝

John 14:6 "Jesus answered, "I am the way and the truth and the life. No one comes to the Father except through me.

Today, lead someone to Christ. Everyone needs Christ in order to get to God. Without Jesus, they will not know the way, the truth or the life of being with God. It is you that can lead them to it all. Take a moment and share the Lord today.

DAY 180

✠

Matthew 11:28 "Come to me, all you who are weary and burdened, and I will give you rest."

Today, if you feel weary and burdened, give it to God. He will give you rest. His arms and shoulders are strong enough to carry all of your burdens. Give it all to him. You are not in this alone in this world and things that you encounter. God is with you.

DAY 181

✝

Colossians 3:12 "Therefore, as God's chosen people, holy and dearly loved, clothe yourselves with compassion, kindness, humility, gentleness and patience."

Today, you are covered with compassion, kindness, humility, gentleness and patience because you are chosen. God has chosen you to do his work. He has chosen you to be his child. Go out with a purpose today. Fulfill all that God's has for you.

DAY 182

✝

John 14:27 "Peace I leave with you; my peace I give you. I do not give to you as the world gives. Do not let your hearts be troubled and do not be afraid."

Today, you have peace because God gives it to you. Your heart will not be troubled or afraid. Let that peace guide you and keep you today and always.

DAY 183

✝

Isaiah 53:4 "Surely he took up our infirmities and carried our sorrows, yet we considered him stricken by God, smitten by him, and afflicted."

Today, even if your body is sick, know that God has put down all that could afflict your body. You are well because you say you are well. He will keep you and protect you. Speak that into the atmosphere today. Claim healing over your body. Claim healing over your mind. Claim the victory in you life now!

DAY 184

✟

Matthew 22:37 "Jesus replied 'Love the Lord your God with all your heart and with all your soul and with your entire mind."

Today, love the Lord with everything that you are and all that you will be. He is the reason you are here today. Be thankful that you woke up this morning. Be thankful that He has given you another opportunity to get it done. Be thankful that you are not the person you were yesterday. Relish in the fact that each day you get better and better. Praise God for who He is and all He has done and will continue to do in your life.

DAY 185

✞

Proverbs 10:4 "Lazy hands make for poverty, but diligent hands bring wealth."

Nothing in life is just handed to you. You have to work hard for every legitimate thing. Stop being lazy. Stop expecting a handout. Strive for more. Strive for better. Get up, get out and make today the best day yet. You won't get rich sitting around without ambition and without endeavors. There is more to you then what you see. Get and go get it. Go get everything you want. Today is the day to ensure laziness ends here.

DAY 186

✝

1 King 18:21 "And Elijah came unto all the people, and said, how long halt ye between two opinions? If the LORD be God, follow him: but if Baal, then follow him. And the people answered him not a word."

Today, know that you have to take a stand on one side or the other. You cannot be in the middle, straddling the fence. Know who you serve and which side you are on. You can stand better on one side or the other but not in the middle. Take a stand. Either you are for God or against Him. Understand in everything that you do you will have to make a stand on one side or the other.

DAY 187

✟

John 6:40 "For this is My Father's will and His purpose, that everyone who sees the Son and believes in and leaves to and trusts in and relies on Him should have eternal life, and I will raise him up [from the dead] at the last day."

Today, know that the will of your heavenly father is that you shall have eternal life with Him and be raised up with Him, even after death. If you believe, then you will have eternal life. Live today in anticipation of living with Him forever.

DAY 188

✟

Ecclesiastes 9:10 "Whatsoever thy hand findeth to do, do it with thy might; for there is no work, nor device, nor knowledge, nor wisdom, in the grave, whither thou goest.

Today, whatever you do today, do it to your best. Do it with a spirit of excellence. Do not do it with a half heart or with little effort. Always do it as best you can. God has given you the ability to do anything you want. Go ahead and go after what it is that you want and give it all you have.

DAY 189

✞

Psalm 57:2 "I will cry to God Most High, Who performs on my behalf and rewards me [Who brings to pass His purposes for me and surely completes them]!

Today, when you cry out to the Most High God, He will work on your behalf and reward you. Go to God and He will complete them for you. Bring it all to Him and watch Him work it out for you.

DAY 190

✝

Mark 14:38 "Watch and pray so that you will not fall into temptation. The spirit is willing, but the flesh is weak."

Today, begin your day with prayer. The flesh is weak and easy to fall to the temptations of the world. Your spirit wants to prevail and overcome the desires of your flesh. Your spirit wants to say no to the temptations. Pray for strength today. No one knows what temptation lies ahead, but pray for the strength of the Lord to resist all temptations.

DAY 191

✞

2 Corinthians 3:18 "But we all, with open face beholding as in a glass the glory of the Lord, are changed into the same image from glory to glory, even as by the Spirit of the Lord."

Today, know that you have been changed when looking at yourself. You are not the person that you were before. The Lord has made you a new creature in the image of the Lord. Receive it and acknowledge you are not what you were before, thanks to the Lord.

DAY 192

✝

Psalm 17:3 "You have proved my heart; you have visited me in the night; you have tried me and find nothing [no evil purpose in me]; I have purposed that my mouth shall not transgress."

Today, you may be tested, but know that your heart is pure and there is no evil in you. You will not speak any evil. You will not do evil. The Lord is with you always. He guides you. He keeps you safe in his arms. Turn to Him when tested today and He will continue to prove your heart pure.

DAY 193

✝

Philippians 2:5 "Let this same attitude and purpose and [humble] mind be in you who were in Christ Jesus: [Let Him be your example in humility:]"

Today, have the right mind and attitude that was in Jesus Christ. He is the example. He is your example. Live like Christ lived. Maintain a positive attitude and humble mind. Then, watch what God begins to do in your life.

DAY 194

✝

1 Corinthians 13:4-7 "Love is patient and kind; love does not envy or boast; it is not arrogant or rude. It does not insist on its own way; it is not irritable or resentful; it does not rejoice at wrong doing, but rejoices with the truth. Love bears all things, believes all things, hopes all things, endure all things."

Today, this scripture says it all. When you have love, you are patient and kind. Love can bear the weight when people are rude, resentful and envy. Love can hold you up with all things that may come your way. Understand that you have that love from God every single day. His love is unwavering. The love that you receive from the world and give to the world should strive to be the kind of love you get from God, unconditional love.

DAY 195

✝

James 4:2 "You desire but do not have, so you kill. You covet but you cannot get what you want, so you quarrel and fight. You do not have because you do not ask God."

Today, if you desire and want something and have not received it, all you have to do is ask the Lord for it. It is just that simple. Just ask.

DAY 196

✝

2 Corinthians 8:8 "I am not commanding you, but I want to test the sincerity of your love by comparing it with the earnestness of others."

Today, you may be tested on your love for God. Your love and faith may be tried at work or in a friendly gathering. Stand stronger than the others. Let your love for God prevail at all times.

DAY 197

✞

Proverbs 12:17 "An honest witness tells the truth, but a false witness tells lies."

Today, and every day you must be person that is honest. Tell the truth always, no matter how you fear the outcome will be. No matter what the truth is. Telling a lie is never a good option. God loves the truth and so will others.

DAY 198

✟

Colossians 3:9-11 "Do not lie to one another, since you have put off the old man with his deeds, and have put on the new man who is renewed in knowledge according to the image of Him who created him, where there is neither Greek nor Jew, circumcised nor uncircumcised, barbarian, Scythian, slave nor free, but Christ is all and in all."

Today and everyday do not lie to other people. You have been transformed from the old you because you are no longer the old person you were. You have been born again new in Christ.

DAY 199

✝

Ecclesiastes 3:17 "I said in my heart, God will judge the righteous and the wicked, for there is a time [appointed] for every matter and purpose and for every work."

Today, do not worry about what is happening or what people are saying because God will judge everyone. There will be those individuals that talk behind your back and smile in your face, but God will handle that. Just focus on what you are supposed to be doing and He will direct your path without hesitation.

DAY 200

✟

Hebrews 10:38 "Now the just shall live by faith: but if any man draws back, my soul shall have no pleasure in him."

Today, live by faith. Do not withdraw from the Lord. The Lord is here for you. Turn to Him, and lean on Him. Let Him guide you. Let Him restore your faith. Let your soul have pleasure with the Lord through your faith. Turning away from Him will give you nothing in return.

DAY 201

✞

Proverbs 4:25 "Let your eyes look right on [with fixed purpose], and let your gaze be straight before you."

What is your purpose? Today, keep your eyes looking straight ahead and not to the right or to the left. You will see clearly. Look with a purpose and watch what happens next.

DAY 202

✝

Proverbs 10:11 "The mouth of a righteous man is a well of life: but violence covereth the mouth of the wicked."

Today, the words from your mouth are full of life because you are righteous. Violence is spoken from the wicked or unrighteous. Negativity reigns from those that are unrighteous. Be like God and be righteous. Do not let evil or things of the ungodly fall from your mouth. Send positivity into the atmosphere with your words. By doing this, you will be closer to God.

DAY 203

✟

Matthew 5:11-12 "Blessed are you when people insult you, persecute you and falsely say all kinds of evil against you because of me. Rejoice and be glad, because great is your reward in heaven, for in the same way they persecuted the prophets who were before you."

The enemy will rear its ugly head today. He will try to come after you in ways you will be shocked to see. But understand that you are blessed. You are a child of God and those that come after will not succeed against you. You must find the strength in knowing that what ever comes against you, your reward lies in heaven and God will see you through.

DAY 204

✝

1 Corinthians 6:18 "Flee from sexual immorality. All other sins a person commits are outside the body, but whoever sins sexually, sins against their own body."

Today, remember to run from sexual desires because it causes the body to sin. Do not indulge in or allow yourself to become unholy by relishing in sexual sin. Keep your body holy. Keep it pure and free from sexual sin. Yes, your flesh is weak. You have the strength and the power to overcome any weakness by keeping God first.

DAY 205

✞

Galatians 1:3-4 "Grace and spiritual blessing be to you and [soul] peace from God the Father and our Lord Jesus Christ (the Messiah), who gave (yielded) Himself up [to atone] for our sins [and to save and sanctify us], in order to rescue and deliver us from this present wicked age and world order, in accordance with the will and purpose and plan of our God and Father."

Today, this is a prayer for you. This prayer is a prayer of Grace and blessings because you are in the will, the purpose and the plan of God. May God's peace continue to be upon you always.

DAY 206

✝

1 Corinthians 15:33 "Do not be misled: 'Bad company corrupts good character.'"

Today, watch the company that you keep around you. If you surround yourself with positive people, positivity is what you will give off. If you surround yourself with negative people, negativity is what you will give off. Moods are contagious. To live a happier life, you must surround yourself with happy people. Indulging in anything less will only corrupt your good character.

DAY 207

✟

Isaiah 42:6 "I the Lord have called you [the Messiah] for a righteous purpose and in righteousness; I will take you by the hand and will keep you; I will give you for a covenant to the people [Israel], for a light to the nations [Gentiles]."

Today, the Lord has you by the hand and is keeping you as He did with the children of Israel and the Gentiles. You have been called for a purpose. Today, become focused on your purpose. You were meant to have it all and to live a life of abundance.

DAY 208

✝

Matthew 18:21-22 "Then Peter came to Jesus and asked, "Lord, how many times shall I forgive my brother or sister who sins against me? Up to seven times?" Jesus answered, "I tell you, not seven times, but seventy-seven times."

Today, forgiveness begins with you and then extends to others. What you must understand is that there is no limit to the amount of times you are to forgive an offense toward you. Jesus says seventy-seven times. It seems so crazy to hear such a thing. However, what is being relayed here is that true forgiveness has no limits. Forgive now, forgive later, then you must forgive again. Once you have finished forgiving then forgive again.

DAY 209

✟

Psalm 107:19 "Then they cried out to the LORD in their trouble, And He saved them out of their distresses."

Today, talk to the Lord for all that bothers you. He will move those things out of your way. He will heal what causes you trouble. He will save you from all that distresses you. Just turn whatever it is over to the Lord.

DAY 210

✝

Ephesians 5:15 "Look carefully then how you walk! Live purposefully and worthily and accurately, not as the unwise and witless, but as wise (sensible, intelligent people)."

Today, and every day, you will walk, talk and live your life with a purpose and full of wisdom. It is the only way to get everything you want.

DAY 211

✞

Philippians 1: 9-10 "And this is my prayer: that your love may abound more and more in knowledge and depth of insight, so that you may be able to discern what is best and may be pure and blameless for the day of Christ."

Today, know that this prayer is for you. This prayer is for you to present yourself faultless unto God. In order for that to occur, the prayer is for love to increase more and more with your knowledge. The prayer is for you to be able to discern what is best. As you learn more, you grow more and thus are able to love more. Your mistakes will become less. You will be pleasing to God.

DAY 212

✝

Isaiah 46:10 "Declaring the end and the result from the beginning, and from ancient times the things that are not yet done, saying, My counsel shall stand, and I will do all My pleasure and purpose."

Today, God has spoken in good counsel and wisdom that He would do good things with a purpose. You must understand that God has a plan and a purpose for you and your life. Talk to Him before moving forward today.

DAY 213

✝

Solomon 2:7 "Oh, let me warn you, sisters in Jerusalem, by the gazelles, yes, by all the wild deer: Don't excite love, don't stir it up, until the time is ripe—and you're ready."

Today, understand that love must come naturally. Do not attempt to stir, and excite it until you are ready. Let love take it's natural course in your life. You will know when you are ready.

DAY 214

✝

Romans 14:9 "For Christ died and lived again for this very purpose, that He might be Lord both of the dead and of the living."

Today, like Christ, you have power over all things dead and alive because Christ lives in you. He died so you could be free and He lives for you too.

DAY 215

✝

1 Corinthians 6:13 "You say, 'Food for the stomach and the stomach for food, and God will destroy them both.' The body, however, is not meant for sexual immorality but for the Lord, and the Lord for the body."

Yes, God can destroy them both. However your body is now holy and for God's use. Do not dishonor your body. Keep your body holy.

DAY 216

✝

Psalm 138:8 "The LORD will perfect that which concerns me; Your mercy, O LORD, endures forever; Do not forsake the works of your hands."

Today, the Lord will complete what He began in you. He will not leave the work unfinished. Today, know that the Lord will finish what He has started concerning you.

DAY 217

✝

1 Corinthians 2:16 "For who has known or understood the mind (the counsels and purposes) of the Lord so as to guide and instruct Him and give Him knowledge? But we have the mind of Christ (the Messiah) and do hold the thoughts (feelings and purposes) of His heart."

Today, you have the counsel and knowledge that Christ has given you because He has given you the mind of Christ. With the mind of Christ, you can do anything. Don't let anything stop you from going after all that God has for you.

DAY 218

✝

Proverbs 18:24 "A man who has friends must himself be friendly, but there is a friend who sticks closer than a brother."

Today, sit back and evaluate yourself. Are you a true friend? In order to be a true friend you must also be friendly. So today, be the friendly person that everyone knows you can be. Be the true friend that is closer than any brother.

DAY 219

✞

Hebrews 6:13-17 "When God made his promise to Abraham, he backed it to the hilt, putting his own reputation on the line. He said, "I promise that I'll bless you with everything I have—bless and bless and bless!" Abraham stuck it out and got everything that had been promised to him. When people make promises, they guarantee them by appeal to some authority above them so that if there is any question that they'll make good on the promise, the authority will back them up. When God wanted to guarantee his promises, he gave his word, a rock-solid guarantee— God can't break his word. And because his word cannot change, the promise is likewise unchangeable."

Today, remember God's desire for you. In His desires He also has promises. His promises do not change. Stand on his promises. When you think times are really hard and rough, remember God's promises. Remember that he is with you always.

DAY 220

✟

Proverbs 13:11 "Dishonest money dwindles away, but whoever gathers money little by little makes it grow."

Today, remember that if you make your money honestly, no matter how small the amount may be God will make it grow. If you get it dishonestly, it will disappear.

DAY 221

✞

Proverbs 16:4 "The Lord has made everything [to accommodate itself and contribute] to its own end and His own purpose--even the wicked [are fitted for their role] for the day of calamity and evil."

Today, know that the Lord your God has made everything, even the wicked for His glory. He will judge us all. Everyone has a purpose and place in God's time.

DAY 222

✝

Romans 8:18 "For I consider that the sufferings of this present time are not worth comparing with the glory that is to be revealed to us."

Today, don't even think about the suffering, physical pain or financial situation that you are in because it cannot compare to your future in God. He has so much planned for you. Get ready. It is on its way.

DAY 223

✝

Isaiah 25:1 "O LORD, You are my God; I will exalt You, I will praise Your name, for You have done wonderful things, even purposes planned of old [and fulfilled] in faithfulness and truth."

Today, you must say, "Oh Lord, you are my God and I exalt you. I praise your name. You have done wonderful things for me in faithfulness and truth. I have my life, health and strength because of you." Acknowledge these things to God today.

DAY 224

✝

I Corinthians 14:20 "Brothers and sisters, stop thinking like children. In regard to evil be infants, but in your thinking be adults."

Today, you should stop thinking like children when dealing with bad people. Be mature in your thinking and be mature in your actions. Do not let other bring you down to their level.

DAY 225

✝

Ephesians 1:5 "For He foreordained us (destined us, planned in love for us) to be adopted (revealed) as His own children through Jesus Christ, in accordance with the purpose of His will [because it pleased Him and was His kind intent]."

Today, understand that if you are not a Jew, then God has made a way through Jesus Christ for you to become a part of His purpose and will because it is His will and intent.

DAY 226

✟

Luke 6:27 "But I say to you who hear: Love your enemies, do good to those who hate you."

Today, hear these words, love your enemies and do good to those we call haters. The haters you will have among you. Love them anyway. They have no stake in what God has for you unless you give it to them.

DAY 227

✞

Proverbs 29:23 "A man's pride will bring him down, but he whose spirit is without pride will receive honor."

Today, you will receive honor because your spirit is without pride. Going forward don't let pride keep you from what God has for you. Continue to receive His honor.

DAY 228

✝

Isaiah 14:24 "The Lord of hosts has sworn, saying, Surely, as I have thought and planned, so shall it come to pass, and as I have purposed, so shall it stand."

Today, know that your words are powerful and what you think and say shall come to pass. Today, choose to speak words that are positive and not negative. Choose to speak words the uplift instead of tear down. Choose to speak as Jesus spoke.

DAY 229

✞

Proverbs 16:28 "A bad man spreads trouble. One who hurts people with bad talk separates good friends."

Today is another day for you to remember people can and will talk bad about you to try and separate you for your friends. Trouble comes from bad men and women. Don't let someone who spreads trouble tear you from your friends.

DAY 230

✞

Proverbs 4:5-7 "Get wisdom! Get understanding! Do not forget, nor turn away from the words of my mouth. Do not forsake her, and she will preserve you; Love her, and she will keep you. Wisdom is the principal thing; therefore get wisdom. And in all your getting, get understanding.

There is security in wisdom, knowledge and understanding. Seek after all. With wisdom, you can gain everything you want. You can gain everything you need. Never stop learning. Never stop seeking after and thirsting after knowledge. Wisdom will give you power. Wisdom will lead you to purpose. Wisdom will guide you when nothing else can guide you. Wisdom will secure you when nothing else will secure you. With wisdom you then gain the understanding. With understanding, everything will all make sense. Everything will come together. Begin today. Don't let anything keep you from gaining wisdom, knowledge and understanding.

DAY 231

✞

Proverbs 13:20 "Whoever walks with the wise becomes wise, but the companion of fools will suffer harm."

Today, you are wise, and let the ones that walk with you become wise. Keeping fools in your company will only bring you harm. Remember you are the sum total of the five closest people to you. What are you doing to surround yourself with success? What are you doing to surround yourself with like-minded individuals? What are you doing to ensure you are constantly improving? What are you doing to ensure you will turn your dreams into reality?

DAY 232

✝

1 John 2:17 "And the world passes away and disappears, and with it the forbidden cravings (the passionate desires, the lust) of it; but he who does the will of God and carries out His purposes in his life abides (remains) forever."

Today, know that after this life passes away, because you are in His will and doing His purpose, you will abide in Christ forever.

DAY 233

✝

Exodus 9:16 "But for this very purpose have I let you live, that I might show you my power, and that My name may be declared throughout all the earth."

Today, you live because of God's power. You can see His power and you can declare His name everywhere you go.

DAY 234

✝

Proverbs 11:13 "He who is always telling stories makes secrets known, but he who can be trusted keeps a thing hidden."

Today, be one of those individuals that people can trust to keep a secret. Don't be the one that gossips. Gossipers can never be trusted. They can turn on you in a minute. When someone comes to you in confidence, keep that confidence. Show them you are someone that can be trusted to keep a secret.

A DAILY DEVOTIONAL

DAY 235

✠

Proverbs 20:18 "Every purpose is established by counsel: and with good advice make war.

Today, good advice comes from good counsel and plans. Preparation is everything. So get ready for what God is about to bring you into.

DAY 236

✞

Leviticus 18:22 "You shall not lie with a male as with a woman. It is an abomination."

Today, remember that God created man and woman. He created them to be together. In God's eyes anything other than this, is an abomination and a sin that separates you from God.

DAY 237

✞

Acts 11:23 "When he arrived and saw the wonderful things God was doing, he was filled with excitement and joy, and encouraged the believers to stay close to the Lord, whatever the cost.

Today, when you see the good favor that God is giving to you and others, be full of joy and encourage others to stay with the Lord, and remain faithful. Have a heart of purpose. Stay close to the Lord no matter what it takes.

DAY 238

✝

Proverbs 17:17 "A true friend is always loyal, and a brother is born to help in time of need."

Today, be a true friend. Be someone who helps in time of need. Be the person that God would have you to be, someone one who is loyal, and someone who is there for anyone that may need you, someone that everyone considers a true friend. Be the friend I know you can be.

DAY 239

✝

Ephesians 5:1-2 "Follow God's example in everything you do just as a much loved child imitates his father. Be full of love for others, following the example of Christ who loved you and gave himself to God as a sacrifice to take away your sins. And God was pleased, for Christ's love for you was like sweet perfume to him."

Today, be full of love for others. Just as Christ was your example spreading love where ever he went, do the same. God will be pleased with you. Imitate God the Father as a child would imitate his parents.

DAY 240

✝

Colossians 1:20 "And God purposed that through (by the service, the intervention of) Him [the Son] all things should be completely reconciled back to Himself, whether on earth or in heaven, as through Him, [the Father] made peace by means of the blood of His cross."

Today, know that God has reconciled you back unto Him through Jesus' blood on the cross. Know that all things have to come back to God to make it complete. You become complete when you accept Jesus Christ as your Lord and Savior. That doesn't mean you become perfect. It means you are now back together with God.

DAY 241

✝

1 John 4:11-12 "Dear friends, since God loved us as much as that, we surely ought to love each other too. For though we have never yet seen God, when we love each other God lives in us, and his love within us grows ever stronger."

Today, is the best day because you know that God loved you so much that you can now love others in the same manner. Even though you have not seen God yet, you love Him and His love that is inside us grows for each other as at grows with Him.

DAY 242

✝

Proverbs 15:22 "Where there is no counsel, purposes are frustrated, but with many counselors they are accomplished."

Today, you need to have good advice and structure. Today, you will need it. Someone will ask you for advice today. You must be prepared to guide them as the Lord would have you to be.

DAY 243

✝

Proverbs 22:6 "Train up a child in the way he should go, And when he is old he will not depart from it."

Today, remember the training you received when you were a child. The Word is within you and always will be there. It never leaves you. You know what you should be doing. You know the plans that God has for you. Focus on his word and you will receive clarity in all areas.

DAY 244

✟

1 Peter 1:22 "Now you can have real love for everyone because your souls have been cleansed from selfishness and hatred when you trusted Christ to save you; so see to it that you really do love each other warmly, with all your hearts."

Today, there is so much love in your heart for each other because you have been cleansed from selfishness and hatred from the day that Christ saved you. His sacrifice has made you a new creature in Him. Act like it. Be the light of the Lord today and every day.

DAY 245

✝

Deuteronomy 31:8 "The LORD himself goes before you and will be with you; he will never leave you nor forsake you. Do not be afraid; do not be discouraged."

Today, have no fear because the Lord will go before you and will be with you in everything you do. He will never leave you or forsake you. Be encouraged. Know that God has your back.

DAY 246

✝

1 John 4:18 "There is no fear in love. But perfect love drives out fear, because fear has to do with punishment. The one who fears is not made perfect in love."

Today, remember that only perfect love can and will drive out fear. If you hold onto fear then you have no perfect love.

DAY 247

✝

Titus 3:4-6 "But when the kindness and love of God our Savior appeared, he saved us, not because of righteous things we had done, but because of his mercy. He saved us through the washing of rebirth and renewal by the Holy Spirit, whom he poured out on us generously through Jesus Christ our Savior."

Today, you are saved through the rebirth and renewal of the Holy Spirit. Live each day to the fullest. Show the world that you belong to Jesus Christ. Show the world that life without Christ is no life at all. People are watching you, even when you think that they are not.

DAY 248

✟

Mark 12:30 "Love the Lord your God with all your heart and with all your soul and with all your mind and with all your strength"

Every single day you must love the Lord with everything you are and have. That is the love that He has for you.

DAY 249

✞

2 Corinthians 9:8 "And God is able to bless you abundantly, so that in all things at all times, having all that you need, you will abound in every good work."

Today, remember that you are abundantly blessed. You are blessed beyond anything you could think of. Be grateful for what you have and how He moves to give you more.

DAY 250

✝

Matthews 10:28 "Do not be afraid of those who kill the body but cannot kill the soul. Rather, be afraid of the One who can destroy both soul and body in hell."

You do not have to fear anyone here on this earth because all they can do is destroy your body. Know this one thing, fear the Lord God almighty because He can destroy your body and soul. Any other fear, just turn it over to the Lord and watch Him work.

DAY 251

✝

Romans 4:21 "Being fully persuaded that God had power to do what he had promised."

You can say completely without a doubt that God had power to what He promised. His word is true and it will never lie. Hold on to the promises He gives you in his word. Know that God has the power to do all the He has promised in your life today and every day.

DAY 252

✝

Romans 16:25-27 "I commit you to God, who is able to make you strong and steady in the Lord, just as the Gospel says, and just as I have told you. This is God's plan of salvation for you Gentiles, kept secret from the beginning of time. But now as the prophets foretold and as God commands, this message is being preached everywhere, so that people all around the world will have faith in Christ and obey him. To God, who alone is wise, be the glory forever through Jesus Christ our Lord. Amen."

Today, step out on faith and spread the message of God's love and plans for His people. Lead those that have strayed from God. Show others the right way to do things. Show them with God at the forefront of everything that you do, that nothing is impossible.

DAY 253

✝

1 Peter 4:11 "Are you called to preach? Then preach as though God himself were speaking through you. Are you called to help others? Do it with all the strength and energy that God supplies so that God will be glorified through Jesus Christ—to him be glory and power forever and ever. Amen"

Whatever you are called to do, whatever your purpose is, you must do it to the glory of God. You may be a preacher, teacher or a helper. Give God the Glory. Keep Him in front of you always. Show others his power. Show others His glory and his might. Glorify Him through Jesus Christ today.

DAY 254

✝

Philippians 2:3-4 "Don't be selfish; don't live to make a good impression on others. Be humble, thinking of others as better than yourself. Don't just think about your own affairs, but be interested in others, too, and in what they are doing."

Today, be humble and think about others more than yourself. Take interest in others and what they do. Let them know that you care. Don't be selfish. Don't be rude. Take an interest in the people around you. It will go a long way today.

DAY 255

✞

Romans 8:26-27 "In the same way the Spirit also helps our weakness; for we do not know how to pray as we should, but the Spirit Himself intercedes for us with groanings too deep for words; and He who searches the hearts knows what the mind of the Spirit is, because He intercedes for the saints according to the will of God."

When you think you know what to pray for and how to pray, know that the spirit intercedes for you. Pray with a mind that it will happen for you. Your prayer may not be perfect, but the spirit is there interceding with God on your behalf.

DAY 256

✞

Matthews 5:44 "But I tell you, love your enemies and pray for those who persecute you,"

Today, know that everyone is not on your side. Even still, you should love everyone anyway. Show your enemies that you are not like them. Show them the love that God has for you. Let it radiate through you and onto them.

DAY 257

✞

Luke 6:28 "bless those who curse you, pray for those who mistreat you."

Have you ever heard the phrase "kill them with kindness"? That is what you must do today. Love them, bless them and treat them the way you want to be treated, regardless of the way they treat you. In fact, you should pray for those that do mistreat you. God can change any situation around including the situations where others mistreat you. Love them anyway.

DAY 258

2 Samuel 7:28 "Now, O Lord GOD, You are God, and Your words are truth, and You have promised this good thing to Your servant."

Today, remember that the Lord is your God and his words are the truth. He has promised good things to you because you are his servant. Live a life of serving others and you will be rewarded beyond measure.

DAY 259

✝

Romans 3:4 "Of course not! Though everyone else in the world is a liar, God is not. Do you remember what the book of Psalms says about this? That God's words will always prove true and right, no matter who questions them."

Today, just like yesterday, God and his word is the truth. He is not a liar. He promised it in the olden days of Psalms and His word is still the same today for you. His words are true and right. Remember that today. No matter who comes at you and questions it that is the truth.

DAY 260

✝

John 4:23-24 "Yet a time is coming and has now come when the true worshipers will worship the Father in the Spirit and in truth, for they are the kind of worshipers the Father seeks. God is spirit, and his worshipers must worship in the Spirit and in truth."

Today, think about this, the time has come for the worshippers to worship God in Spirit and in truth. God is a spirit. The father is seeking those that follow Him and seek Him in the Spirit. Worship Him now. Worship Him with a whole heart and worship Him in truth.

DAY 261

✝

Romans 1:18 "For the wrath of God is revealed from heaven against all ungodliness and unrighteousness of men, who suppress the truth in unrighteousness

Today, be mindful that God's wrath will come against the ungodliness and unrighteousness of mankind, those who deny the truth. You know the truth. Don't let anyone turn you against what you know is right.

DAY 262

✞

Titus 2:7-8 "In all things showing yourself to be a pattern of good works; in doctrine showing integrity, reverence, incorruptibility, sound speech that cannot be condemned, that one who is an opponent may be ashamed, having nothing evil to say of you."

Today, show that you are a person of good works. Show everyone that God lives inside of you. Let them see it in the way that you dress. Let them see it in the way that you walk and the way that you talk. Do not be ashamed of Him. Let everyone know how good God is and has been to you.

DAY 263

✝

1 Kings 17:24 "Then the woman said to Elijah, "Now by this I know that you are a man of God, and that the word of the LORD in your mouth is the truth."

Today, as well as each and every day, tell people the truth. People will know that you are a man or woman of God because what you have told them is the truth. Never tell a lie to them. Integrity lies in the words that come out of your mouth. What do you want the world to hear?

DAY 264

✝

Job 27:4 "My lips will not say anything wicked, and my tongue will not utter lies."

Be the person that doesn't utter lies. Stand for what is right. Speak what is right, no matter how hard it may seem to be. You have to be that person that does the right thing, that person that tells the truth at all times. Start today with no lies. Today, you can say "with my lips and tongue I will speak the truth and will not lie."

DAY 265

✝

Galatians 4:16 "Have I now become your enemy by telling you the truth?"

Today, you may become the enemy of your coworkers or family members just because you are speaking the truth. Don't let that stop you or deter you from speaking the truth. God will smile upon you for the truth.

DAY 266

✝

1 Timothy 1:5 "The goal of this command is love, which comes from a pure heart and a good conscience and a sincere faith."

Today, have a pure heart and a conscious mind with sincere faith to do God's will. When you speak today do it with a pure heart and mind. Everyone will not do that. Take notice of those with an impure heart and make a commitment today to be one that is pure in all that you. No hidden agenda. No ultimatum. Be someone who has pure love for Christ in everything that you do. There will be those around you that will have a hidden agenda. There will be those with an impure heart. Be careful, be watchful, and remain faithful. When you have a pure heart, good conscience and sincere faith, you have LOVE.

DAY 267

✝

Acts 20:35 "In everything I did, I showed you that by this kind of hard work we must help the weak, remembering the words the Lord Jesus himself said: 'It is more blessed to give than to receive.' "

Today, begin the day by doing something nice for someone else. Too often we go through the hustle of the day without taking the time to do something extra for someone else. We rush through our schedule and daily lives not thinking of anyone that is not immediate to us. It's time to do something extra. I'm not talking about doing something extra for someone you know. I'm talking about doing something extra without being asked to do it. Do something extra for someone you don't know. Take the challenge and give something to someone who would not have otherwise had it. Make today the start of doing something for someone always.

DAY 268

✝

1 John 3:18 "Little children, let us not love with word or with tongue, but in deed and truth."

Today is about being a person of action. It's one thing to say you are living for God. It is a totally different thing to show that you are living for God. Everything you say today shows it in your actions. Don't just say you love someone with your mouth. Show them with your actions. Show them through what you will do for them. Remember, actions speak louder than words.

DAY 269

✝

Romans 14:1 "Accept the one whose faith is weak, without quarreling over disputable matters."

Today, you will find someone that is weak in the Lord. There is no need to argue with them. Uplift them with your words of wisdom. Encourage them to stay the course. Acknowledge them and let them know God is in control. Spread the love of God to anyone you meet.

DAY 270

✝

Romans 15:1-2 "We who are strong ought to bear with the failings of the weak and not to please ourselves. Each of us should please our neighbors for their good, to build them up."

Today, lift up your neighbors and family. They may be going though hard times. You can be their strength. You can be the light that brings them out of the darkness. You can be the strength that moves them from weakness. You are strong. Share your strength.

DAY 271

✝

Philippians 3:15 "Therefore let us, as many as are mature, have this mind; and if in anything you think otherwise, God will reveal even this to you."

Today, your mind is strong. If the enemy was to try to make you doubt it, God will reveal to you just how strong your mind is. Today, don't doubt it. Don't doubt your strength.

DAY 272

✝

James 5:19-20 "My brothers and sisters, if one of you should wander from the truth and someone should bring that person back, remember this: Whoever turns a sinner from the error of their way will save them from death and cover over a multitude of sins."

We have all been called to spread the gospel of Jesus Christ. In doing so, we are saving lives. Sharing the gospel does lead people to Christ. Begin today. Lead people to Christ, one soul at a time.

DAY 273

✟

1 John 3:15 "Anyone who hates a brother or sister is a murderer, and you know that no murderer has eternal life residing in him"

Today, do not allow yourself to harbor hate for anyone. God does not promise eternal life with Him in heaven if you continue to hate one another. You must let it go. Let go of all things not of God.

DAY 274

✝

Matthew 5:8 "Blessed are the pure in heart: for they shall see God."

Do you have a pure heart? Today, understand that God is searching for those with a pure heart. He is searching for someone who is after his own heart. In order to be a person after God's own heart, your heart must be pure. Don't let the negativity of others deter you from what God has for you. Seek after him and he will lead you to everything your heart desires. What you must understand is that when our hearts become aligned with God's heart, then we stop thinking of ourselves and start thinking of others. The selfishness ends. Others become our priority. Be the man or the woman that is after God's own heart. Be someone that has a pure heart.

DAY 275

✝

Romans 5:1-2 "Therefore, since we have been justified by faith, we have peace with God through our Lord Jesus Christ. Through him we have also obtained access by faith into this grace in which we stand, and we rejoice in hope of the glory of the God.

Today, you are justified by faith and have peace through Jesus. With this faith, you can stand and rejoice in His glory. Nothing can stop you. Go after your dreams, visions and aspirations. Rejoice, for everything is coming your way in the hope of his glory.

DAY 276

✝

Proverbs 2:2-4 "turning your ear to wisdom and applying your heart to understanding indeed, if you call out for insight and cry aloud for understanding, and if you look for it as for silver and search for it as for hidden treasure."

Today, listen for wisdom and understanding for your heart. Seek for it like you are looking for a hidden treasure of silver and gold. Seek it.

DAY 277

✝

Proverbs 3:13-14 "Blessed are those who find wisdom, those who gain understanding, for she is more profitable than silver and yields better returns than gold."

Today, you will find wisdom and understanding. They are better than silver and gold. Don't let the wisdom pass you by. Don't overlook it or toss it aside. With blessings comes wisdom.

DAY 278

✞

Proverbs 17:5 "Those who mock the poor insult their Maker; those who rejoice at the misfortune of others will be punished."

Today, be careful and not make fun of the poor and misfortune of the others. You may be punished. Instead, reach out to the less fortunate. Focus on helping someone that needs it.

DAY 279

✝

Proverbs 17:16 "It is senseless to pay tuition to educate a fool, since he has no heart for learning."

Today, education is great. Remember the teaching of the Bible and learn with your heart, mind and spirit. The teaching in the bible will guide you through any obstacle in your life.

DAY 280

✞

Proverbs 8:10 "Choose my instruction instead of silver, knowledge rather than choice gold."

Today, you should choose God's word and follow his instruction and knowledge rather than silver and gold. Like the song says, "I'd rather have Jesus than silver and gold."

A DAILY DEVOTIONAL

DAY 281

✝

Proverbs 22:2 "The rich and poor have this in common: The Lord made them both."

Today, remember the Lord God made everything and everyone, rich and poor. Today, do not treat others different because they have something or they do not have something. Treat everyone the same because God made everyone and everything.

DAY 282

✝

Proverbs 28:6 "Better to be poor and honest than to be dishonest and rich."

God wants you to be a person of honesty. It doesn't matter what you have. You must be a person who is honest. God holds honesty so high that He says it is better to be poor and honest rather than be rich and dishonest. Today, you may have money but are you honest?

DAY 283

✝

Proverbs 28:25 "Greed causes fighting; trusting the Lord leads to prosperity."

Today, you have no need to fight others for what they have. Trust the Lord and He will lead you to the prosperity you desire.

DAY 284

✝

Proverbs 3:27 "Do not withhold good from those who deserve it when it's in your power to help them."

Today, help someone. You hold the power in your hands to do good for anyone. Don't keep your good deed from those that deserve it most. Lend a helping hand today and every single day. Try each day to help someone that would not otherwise have that help.

DAY 285

✟

Proverbs 11:4 "Riches won't help on the day of judgment, but right living can save you from death."

Today, and everyday live right and you will be saved from death on the Day of Judgment. When Judgment day comes, it doesn't matter how much money you have, or how big your home is. Accepting Christ as your Lord and savior and living right is the way to eternal life.

DAY 286

✝

Proverbs 22:26-27 "Don't agree to guarantee another person's debt or put up security for someone else. If you can't pay it, even your bed will be snatched from under you."

Today, be careful about taking on someone debts or loans. Don't put up security for them if you can't pay it. You may lose your own valuable things. You must be a good steward of your own finances, even when lending to others.

DAY 287

✝

Proverbs 19:17 "If you help the poor, you are lending to the Lord— and he will repay you!"

Today, when you help the poor, the Lord will repay you. Know that He will reward you for your good deeds now and in heaven. The poor will always be among you. Helping them is pleasing to the Lord.

DAY 288

✝

Proverbs 11:24 "Give freely and become [wealthier]; be stingy and lose everything."

Today, give freely from your heart and more will come back you. Now if you are stingy you can lose everything.

DAY 289

✞

Proverbs 22:9 "Blessed are those who are generous, because they feed the poor."

Today, when you give to the needy, you will be blessed. Be generous with your time, talents and treasures. Take care of those less fortunate. Give back in some way today.

DAY 290

✝

Proverbs 22:4 "True humility and fear of the Lord lead to riches, honor, and long life."

To be humble is to be with the Lord. Today, I want you to humble yourself. I want you to fear the Lord. In order to have a long life full of riches, you must be able to be humble and remain humble.

A DAILY DEVOTIONAL

DAY 291

✢

Proverbs 11:18 "Evil people get rich for the moment, but the reward of the godly will last."

Today, don't worry about the people that have more than you because it is for only a moment. Remain godly and your reward will be one that last forever.

DAY 292

✝

Proverbs 20:13 "If you love sleep, you will end in poverty. Keep your eyes open, and there will be plenty to eat!"

Today, think of this proverb and always be watchful. Don't be lazy today, sleeping your life away. Stay focused. Stay persistent. Keep your eyes open and you will have plenty to eat.

DAY 293

✞

Proverbs 22:1 "Choose a good reputation over great riches; being held in high esteem is better than silver or gold."

You may think people look to have lots of silver and gold but think on this; people should say you have a good reputation.

DAY 294

✝

Proverbs 13:21 "Trouble chases sinners, while blessings reward the righteous."

You should not worry about troubles following you today. Riches and blessings are waiting for you because you are one of the righteous. God rewards the righteous.

DAY 295

✝

Proverbs 21:5 "Good planning and hard work lead to prosperity, but hasty shortcuts lead to poverty."

Today, don't take the short cut on things you are planning. A little hard work won't hurt you. It will lead to your prosperity.

DAY 296

✝

Proverbs 17:7 "Respected people do not tell lies, and fools have nothing worthwhile to say."

Be a person that is respected. Be a person of your word. Without your word, you have nothing. A person that lies is like a fool with nothing to say. Don't fall into foolish ways of living a life of lies and deceit. Be a person that people love, respect, and call honest.

DAY 297

✞

Ephesians 4:29 "Do not let any unwholesome talk come out of your mouths, but only what is helpful for building others up according to their needs, that it may benefit those who listen."

Today, you should speak words that help not hurt people. Building others up is far better than tearing someone down, especially in the eyes of the Lord. Have the character that genuinely cares about others, and thus, your words and actions reveal will same.

DAY 298

✝

John 14:1 "Let not your heart be troubled; you believe in God, believe also in Me."

Jesus' words to you is that you should not be worried or troubled with anything because He wants you to believe in Him, the son of God, the savior of the world.

DAY 299

✝

Acts 4:2 "Being greatly disturbed that they taught the people and preached in Jesus the resurrection from the dead"

As in the Bible days people that don't believe in Jesus and what He did become upset and disturbed when you tell them about how great He is in your life and what He can do for them.

DAY 300

✝

Psalms 103:10-12 "He has not punished us as we deserve for all our sins, for his mercy toward those who fear and honor him is as great as the height of the heavens above the earth. He has removed our sins as far away from us as the east is from the west."

Today, God's mercy endures for us all day after day, month after month, and year after year. His love for us is so great that He sacrificed his son so that our sins could be removed from us and placed as far away as possible. He did that instead of punishing us for those sins. Maintain your fear in Him and honor Him. His mercy is everlasting.

A DAILY DEVOTIONAL

DAY 301

✝

Romans 6:23" For the wages of sin is death, but the free gift of God is eternal life through Jesus Christ our Lord."

You were saved from eternal death when you accepted Christ as your Lord and Savior. Why not save someone else by sharing this gift from God? Today, lead someone to Christ with these words: "The wages of sin is death, but the gift of God is eternal life through Jesus Christ our Lord." Amen.

DAY 302

✞

John 1:12 "But as many as received Him, to them He gave the right to become children of God, to those who believe in His name."

Those that believe in Jesus Christ are made new and are children of the Lord. As a child of God, preach His gospel to everyone you know. Show them the way to God so they too can be children of the Lord.

DAY 303

✞

John 3:3" Jesus answered and said to him, "Most assuredly, I say to you, unless one is born again, he cannot see the kingdom of God"

Today, the kingdom of God is your future because you are born again. You are a true believer in Jesus Christ. You must be born again to see Jesus. Be glad today that you will see Jesus and the kingdom of God.

DAY 304

✝

John 8:32 "And you shall know the truth, and the truth shall make you free."

Today, you know that you have been born again and the truth of the Lord is within you and you are free from sin. Don't let someone or something take that away. Fight hard to remain pure and holy. Fight for the truth. Fight hard to remain free.

DAY 305

✟

John 14:15 "If you love me, keep my commandments."

Today, God is saying to you that if you love Him, you will keep His commandments. He will not steal, kill or destroy. You will not break God's commandments. Keep his commandments and show your love for our heavenly father.

DAY 306

✝

Romans 3:10 "*As it is written: 'There is none righteous, no, not one'*"

Today, you can complete this by knowing that by accepting Jesus Christ as your Lord and Savior, you are born again into righteousness. Without God there is no one righteous.

DAY 307

✝

James 1:2 "Consider it pure joy, my brothers and sisters, whenever you face trials of many kinds"

Today, if you are going through hard times, put a smile on your face. Know that no matter what you are going through, God will see you through. Remember your test is a testimony that will see someone else through.

DAY 308

✝

Matthew 7:21" Not everyone who says to me, 'Lord, Lord,' will enter the kingdom of heaven, but only the one who does the will of my Father who is in heaven."

Today, there are so many people that think as long as they can say Lord or call on His name that it will get them into heaven. Know now that the one that does the will of God will see Him in heaven. It takes more than just calling on the name of Jesus. You have to be like Jesus. Work like Jesus. Pray like Jesus. Live like Jesus.

DAY 309

✝

Matthew 7:8 "For everyone who asks receives; the one who seeks finds; and to the one who knocks, the door will be opened."

Today, understand that you have to go after whatever it is that you want. You won't find it if you are not looking for it. Success waits for no one. Go get your blessing. Ask for your blessing. The door is waiting to be opened. All you have to do is knock at the door.

DAY 310

✝

1 John 2:15 "Do not love the world or anything in the world. If anyone loves the world, love for the Father is not in them."

Remember, this world is no longer the place you can call home. The things in this world are for your temporary use. With the love of the Father the world that He has prepared for you is greater than this world that we live in.

DAY 311

✝

James 1:7 "But let him ask in faith, with no doubting, for he who doubts is like a wave of the sea driven and tossed by the wind. For let not that man suppose that he will receive anything from the Lord;"

When you ask for anything, ask it knowing that it is yours already without any doubt. Your faith cannot bounce up and down and around. You must stand firm in your faith. You be firm. No doubts.

DAY 312

✝

Leviticus 19:18 "Do not seek revenge or bear a grudge against anyone among your people, but love your neighbor as yourself. I am the Lord."

Today, don't think bad or evil about the people you are around, but love them. Don't hold grudges. Let it go. Today, remember this holding on to anything negative will only cause unneeded stress. Let it go. It's just not worth it.

DAY 313

✝

2 Peter 1:5-7 "For this very reason, make every effort to add to your faith goodness; and to goodness, knowledge; and to knowledge, self-control; and to self-control, perseverance; and to perseverance, godliness; and to godliness, mutual affection; and to mutual affection, love."

Today, make every effort to be in control of your faith, goodness, knowledge, self-control, perseverance, godliness, and mutual affection to end anything with love.

DAY 314

✟

1 Corinthians 10:31 "So whether you eat or drink or whatever you do, do it all for the glory of God."

Today, when you eat, drink or do anything, do it to and for the glory of God. Your body is the temple of the Holy Spirit. Everything that you do should glorify God, not just today but every day.

DAY 315

✝

Romans 12:9 "Love must be sincere. Hate what is evil; cling to what is good."

Today, hold fast to God's love and hold on to what is good. If you must hate, then hate what is evil. Evil is the enemy not God and certainly not his love.

DAY 316

✝

Psalms 122:7 "May there be peace within your walls and security within your citadels."

Today, you should claim that you will have peace in your home. Claim that you will have peace in all that surrounds you. Know that God is watching and rest assured that He will protect you.

DAY 317

✝

Matthew 5:38-39 *"You have heard that it was said, 'An eye for an eye and a tooth for a tooth.' But I tell you not to resist an evil person. "But whoever slaps you on your right cheek, turn the other to him also."*

Even though you have heard an eye for an eye and a tooth for a tooth, God is saying to turn your back to that. If someone hits, you disregard it. There is no better way to show that you are the better person than to ignore the wrong that has been done against you.

DAY 318

✝

1 Corinthians 16:14 "Do everything in love."

God is love. He loves you and only wants the best for you. In all things that you do today, you must do those things with love. Work in love. Live in love. Hope in love. Have faith with love. Inspire with love. Promote with love. Reward with love. Remember with love. Let love guide you today.

DAY 319

✝

Matthew 10:37 "Anyone who loves their father or mother more than me is not worthy of me; anyone who loves their son or daughter more than me is not worthy of me."

Today, you must know that God comes first. He comes first in your heart, in your spirit, in mind and in everything that you do. Understand that if you put anything before God including your mother, father, son, daughter or anything, then you are not worthy of God. Be worthy of God. Keep Him first in everything that you do and everything else will fall into place.

DAY 320

✝

Philippians 2:2 "then make my joy complete by being like-minded, having the same love, being one in spirit and of one mind."

Today, be encouraged in the comfort of the Lord by having the same mind and spirit of Him. He is righteous and He wants you to also be righteous. The love He has for you He wants you to have for others.

DAY 321

✝

1 John 4:21 "And he has given us this command: Anyone who loves God must also love their brother and sister."

Today, if you love God then you must love everyone. This is a commandment. Don't let any day pass by without showing the love you have for everyone. Pass the love that you have for God onto others.

DAY 322

✝

Revelations 21:4 "' 'He will wipe every tear from their eyes. There will be no more death' or mourning or crying or pain, for the old order of things has passed away."

Today, have comfort in knowing that God will wipe away all your tears. He is your comforter. He will see you through.

DAY 323

✝

Romans 13:10 "Love does no wrong to anyone. That's why it fully satisfies all of God's requirements. It is the only law you need."

Today, with God's love in you, you will do no wrong to anyone. Love is the way. Since God is love then use love in all that you do. Love is a requirement of God. It should be a requirement of you too.

DAY 324

✝

Zephaniah 3:17 "The LORD your God is with you, the Mighty Warrior who saves. He will take great delight in you; in his love he will no longer rebuke you, but will rejoice over you with singing."

Today, your actions will delight the Lord. He loves you and He has saved you. He rejoices in the things that you do. Take comfort knowing that He is for you and sings praises over you.

A DAILY DEVOTIONAL

DAY 325

✝

Colossians 3:14 "And over all these virtues put on love, which binds them all together in perfect unity."

Today, know that love is the glue that holds everything together in perfect unison. Use it in everything that you do. Be the love that holds everything together.

DAY 326

✝

Proverbs 10:12 "Hatred stirs up conflict, but love covers over all wrongs."

Today, live a life that leaves hatred behind you. Love is what will see you through any conflict that arises. Do not indulge in hateful things. Use the love of the Lord to be the best you can be and to overcome the conflicts that may arise today. Know that haters you will have among you, but love will always prevail.

DAY 327

✝

Psalms 116:1 "I love the L ORD, for he heard my voice; he heard my cry for mercy"

God has heard your cry for mercy. He hears your prayers. He knows your wants and your needs. Love Him as He loves you today. He is there for you.

DAY 328

✝

Isaiah 41:10 "So do not fear, for I am with you; do not be dismayed, for I am your God. I will strengthen you and help you; I will uphold you with my righteous right hand."

God is your God. He will give you strength today and help you through whatever may arise. When you feel like falling, God will hold you up. So don't be afraid today because God is with you always.

DAY 329

✝

John 13:34-35 "A new command I give you: Love one another. As I have loved you, so you must love one another. By this everyone will know that you are my disciples, if you love one another."

You must love one another the way God loves you. Love without judgment, without hurt, without malice or strife. God loves unconditionally and you must love the same way.

DAY 330

✝

John 2:3-4 "And you make a lot of fuss over the rich man and give him the best seat in the house and say to the poor man, "You can stand over there if you like or else sit on the floor"—well, judging a man by his wealth shows that you are guided by wrong motives.

Today, you must treat everyone the same. It doesn't matter if they are rich or poor. It doesn't matter if they have many things or very little. Treat everyone the same. If you treat them different then you are judging and your motives are wrong.

DAY 331

✞

Ephesians 1:3 "Praise be to the God and Father of our Lord Jesus Christ, who has blessed us in the heavenly realms with every spiritual blessing in Christ."

Today, give praise for the blessings that you have from Christ. Those blessings, those that are material and spiritual, all of it, give praise for it. In everything give thanks, especially for those things we will have in heaven.

DAY 332

✟

Luke 13:3 "Not at all! And don't you realize that you also will perish unless you leave your evil ways and turn to God?"

In order to make it in this world, you have to leave everything to God. He is the way. Turn everything that is not of Him away from you and turn to Him. Let Him be your salvation.

DAY 333

✝

Luke 18:9-13 "To some who were confident of their own righteousness and looked down on everyone else, Jesus told this parable: "Two men went up to the temple to pray, one a Pharisee and the other a tax collector. The Pharisee stood by himself and prayed: 'God, I thank you that I am not like other people—robbers, evildoers, adulterers—or even like this tax collector. I fast twice a week and give a tenth of all I get.' "But the tax collector stood at a distance. He would not even look up to heaven, but beat his breast and said, 'God, have mercy on me, a sinner.'"

Today, don't hold yourself higher than anyone else. Acknowledge your faults and know that God will have mercy on you. Do not brag of what you do but remain humble. Be confident, and do not look down on anyone else.

DAY 334

✝

James 4:4 "Adulterers and adulteresses! Do you not know that friendship with the world is enmity with God? Whoever therefore wants to be a friend of the world makes himself an enemy of God."

You are a believer in God. You must remember that God is not of the world. If you put your focus on Him and not of those things that are not Him, you will be a friend of His. Focusing on those things not of Him puts you against God and, therefore, an enemy. Don't be drawn away from God today. Stay focused!

DAY 335

✝

James 1:13 "Let no one say when he is tempted, "I am tempted by God"; for God cannot be tempted by evil, nor does He Himself tempt anyone."

God does not tempt you to do evil things. He is good. He is pure. He has not temptation in Him whatsoever and, therefore, cannot tempt you. Do not blame God when you make a decision to fall for temptation. Accept that you have done wrong, repent and ask for forgiveness. But do not blame God for the temptation.

DAY 336

✝

Hebrews 12:14 "Make every effort to live in peace with everyone and to be holy; without holiness no one will see the Lord."

Today, because you are living in peace and with holiness, it will lead others to the Lord. Remember, salvation is what has saved you and is what will save others. Without holiness, others cannot see the Lord and, therefore, may not be saved.

DAY 337

✝

John 15:12" My command is this: Love each other as I have loved you."

Today, the Lord has commanded us to love each other as He loves us. Today, make every effort to spread that love. Don't limit your love to those that you know. You must love everyone and love them unconditionally. Share your love in everything that you do.

DAY 338

✞

Matthew 18:20 "For where two or three are gathered together in My name, I am there in the midst of them."

Today, when you go to God, go to Him with at least two others. He is in the midst when two or three are gathered in his name. The power that you hold together is what will be needed today.

DAY 339

✝

Matthew 6:1 "Take heed that you do not do your charitable deeds before men, to be seen by them. Otherwise you have no reward from your Father in heaven."

Today, do good to please God. He is the one that you have to please. Man is not the reason for you to do good deeds. If you are doing good deeds to please man, then you are not pleasing in God's eye sight. Your reward is in Him, not man.

DAY 340

✝

Jude 1:2 "Mercy, peace, and love be multiplied to you."

God's mercy, peace and love are with you. Today, it is multiplied. Feel it, accept it, and relish in his love, his peace and his mercy.

DAY 341

✝

Matthew 7:12 "Therefore, whatever you want men to do to you, do also to them, for this is the Law and the Prophets."

If you want someone to be good to you, you must be good to them. Understand the Law of doing to others what you want them to do to you. This is what you must do every single day.

DAY 342

✝

Galatians 6:7 "Do not be deceived, God is not mocked; for whatever a man sows, that he will also reap."

Today, understand that what you do shall be done also to you. Treat people the way you want to be treated. Give out good and good will come back to you. Give out bad and bad will come back to you. You have the power to have your life exactly the way you want it. Ensure you are sending and giving out exactly what you want to get back.

DAY 343

✝

Matthew 7:15 "Beware of false prophets, who come to you in sheep's clothing, but inwardly they are ravenous wolves."

Today, not everyone that you encounter in your life is for you. Some will tell you lies and deceive you while pretending to be for you. They are sheep dressed as wolves and you need to recognize that they do exist.

DAY 344

✝

1 John 1:8 "If we say that we have no sin, we deceive ourselves, and the truth is not in us."

Today, remember no one is perfect and no one is without sin. If you think that you have no sin at all, you are only deceiving yourself. Show your truth. Be honest with yourself. You are not perfect but continue each day to strive for perfection. Live your life to the fullest and put God first. Live as Christ lived and you will get as close to perfection as you can.

DAY 345

✝

Hebrews 10:24 "And let us consider one another in order to stir up love and good works."

Today, the love of the Lord is stirred up within your good works. Think of whom you will help today. Show them the love of the Lord in the good deed(s) that you will do for them today. God is pleased when you do well for others.

DAY 346

✞

John 14:27 "Peace I leave with you. My peace I give to you. I do not give peace to you as the world gives. Do not let your hearts be troubled or afraid."

Today is not the day neither is any day to be filled with fear of any type. Don't let your mind and your heart be filled with the troubles of the world. God's grace is with you. His grace is sufficient to see you through anything. Today, know that there is no fear when it comes to Him. Leave everything that is not of him alone and focus on Him. He will direct you, lead you and guide you.

DAY 347

2 Corinthian 1:2 "Grace to you and peace from God our Father and the Lord Jesus Christ."

Today, begin your day with the understanding that Grace is with you. God's peace will be with you wherever you are and where ever you go. These things have been given to you by God and Jesus Christ. Don't let today end without being grateful for His love, his grace, and his peace.

DAY 348

✝

Galatians 5:16 "I advise you to obey only the Holy Spirit's instructions. He will tell you where to go and what to do, and then you won't always be doing the wrong things your evil nature wants you to."

You have a natural sense in you that make you want to do act badly. That nature wants to lead you in the wrong direction. You have to listen to that still, small voice in your ear. It will keep you from doing wrong and it is called the Holy Spirit.

DAY 349

✝

Acts 17:30 "God did not remember these times when people did not know better. But now He tells all men everywhere to be sorry for their sins and to turn from them."

Today, whatever ways that you have that are wrong, ask for forgiveness. Change those ways and then don't go back to those ways.

DAY 350

✝

Matthew 18:15 "If a brother sins against you, go to him privately and confront him with his fault. If he listens and confesses it, you have won back a brother."

Today, if someone does something against you, go to them. Confront them. Let them know what they have done. If they agree, own up to the wrong doing, and then this relationship can be saved.

DAY 351

✝

Matthews 4:1 "Then Jesus was led out into the wilderness by the Holy Spirit, to be tempted there by Satan."

Today, as each day goes by, do not think that you are immune from temptation. Do not think your significant other is immune from temptation. Do not think anyone is immune from temptation. Even Jesus was tempted by the devil.

DAY 352

✝

Matthew 7:7 "Ask and it will be given to you; seek and you will find; knock and the door will be opened to you."

Today, whatever you need God has it. Whatever the obstacles are that are hindering you from moving forward He can move them out of your way. Whatever you are looking for you will find it. Don't allow doors to remain closed to you today. Knock, and watch God begin to open them for you. Today is the day to turn everything around in your favor.

DAY 353

✟

James 2:14 "Dear brothers, what's the use of saying that you have faith and are Christians if you aren't proving it by helping others? Will that kind of faith save anyone?"

Today, show your faith with your action. Remember, faith without works is dead. You must put your faith into action. Use your faith and help others. Show them how faith works. Showing them your faith will lead them to salvation. You are here to lead others to Christ. Be a Christian that shares Christ. Give your faith, show your faith, be your faith.

DAY 354

✝

James 1:5 "If any of you lacks wisdom, you should ask God, who gives generously to all without finding fault, and it will be given to you."

To have knowledge of what is, all you have to do is ask God for it. He will lead you and guide you and give all the knowledge you need. God is a generous giver. He is generous with his love, his grace, and his mercy. He will also be generous with what you ask for including knowledge.

DAY 355

✟

2 John 1:3 "Grace, mercy and peace from God the Father and from Jesus Christ, the Father's Son, will be with us in truth and love."

You have the free and unmerited favor of God. You have his mercy and his peace. This will be with you always. So go out today and claim what is yours. Expect the unexpected in the truth and love that is Jesus Christ, the Son of God.

DAY 356

✞

Mark 16:16 "Those who believe and are baptized will be saved. But those who refuse to believe will be condemned."

Today, I ask you, "Do you believe you?" If you believe, have you been baptized? If you do not believe, you will be condemned. Don't live the rest of your life without the salvation of the Lord. Don't be condemned.

DAY 357

✞

John 5:24 "Very truly I tell you, whoever hears my word and believes him who sent me has eternal life and will not be judged but has crossed over from death to life."

Because you have heard his words and believed in Him that sent Jesus, you will not be judged. You have crossed over from the Death of this world to eternal life in the other.

DAY 358

✝

Matthew 7:1 "Do not judge, or you too will be judged."

Today, you have to stop being that person that looks at everyone like they can only do wrong. Stop being the person that evaluates a person on what you think is right. Accept people for who they are. That does not mean you cannot teach right from wrong. It does not mean you cannot instruct on what right and wrong is. It does, however, mean that you cannot sit in judgment against someone else. It does mean you cannot be quick to judge the action of others as if you have no wrong in your life. Remember, God is the only true judge.

DAY 359

✝

Ephesians 6:10 "Last of all I want to remind you that your strength must come from the Lord's mighty power within you."

Today, you must realize everything you need to accomplish anything is already in you. No need to turn anywhere else. No need to ask anyone else. The Lord's mighty power is within you and you can do all things with that strength.

DAY 360

✠

John 15: 5 "I am the vine; you are the branches. If you remain in me and I in you, you will bear much fruit; apart from me you can do nothing."

God is the person that will give you everything. He is the vine to your branches. With Him you can do and have anything. If you decide God is not for you, or that you can do without Him, then you will have nothing.

A DAILY DEVOTIONAL

DAY 361

✝

2 Corinthians 5:21 "God made him who had no sin to be sin for us, so that in him we might become the righteousness of God."

God sent his son for you, for me, for everyone. He sacrificed his son who had no sin in Him at all for all of us who were not without sin. Today, realize how big that sacrifice was. Would you sacrifice your child for everyone else who was full of wrong?

DAY 362

✝

Galatians 5:13 "It is absolutely clear that God has called you to a free life. Just make sure that you don't use this freedom as an excuse to do whatever you want to do and destroy your freedom. Rather, use your freedom to serve one another in love; that's how freedom grows."

Understand today that God has given you a freedom like no other. This freedom gives you the ability to make your own decisions. Today, make wise choices. Serve others, learn from others and love others. That is the only way your freedom will grow with God.

DAY 363

†

Joshua 24:15 "But if you are unwilling to obey the Lord, then decide today whom you will obey. Will it be the gods of your ancestors beyond the Euphrates or the gods of the Amorites here in this land? But as for me and my family, we will serve the Lord."

Today, as we come to the end of the year-long devotional, you know you have decided to serve God. You must always make sure that when putting Him first you also let others know that they have a choice of whom they will serve. Serve the Lord with gladness and let everyone see what God can do if they too choose him.

DAY 364

✞

2 Timothy 3:15-17 "and how from infancy you have known the Holy Scriptures, which are able to make you wise for salvation through faith in Christ Jesus. All Scripture is God-breathed and is useful for teaching, rebuking, correcting and training in righteousness, so that the servant of God may be thoroughly equipped for every good work.

Today, don't forget those things that were taught to you when you were young, especially the word of God. God's word is what has prepared you to come to know his son Jesus Christ through salvation. God's word is what will help you each day. God's word will provide you wisdom and give you the ability to do his will.

DAY 365

✟

Psalm 4:12 "Surely, LORD, you bless the righteous; you surround them with your favor as with a shield"

Today, know that those that are righteous are surrounded with God's favor. Today, live with righteousness. Remember to keep God first in all that you do. He is the one to please. In pleasing Him you will gain favor above all.

DAY 366

✝

Bonus:

1 Corinthians 6:9 "Or do you not know that wrongdoers will not inherit the kingdom of God? Do not be deceived: Neither the sexually immoral nor idolaters nor adulterers nor men who have sex with men nor thieves nor the greedy nor drunkards nor slanderers nor swindlers will inherit the kingdom of God."

Today, make the decision to do right. Make the decision to take a stand and accept Jesus as you Lord and Savior. Make the decision today to leave all that is bad behind in pursuit of all that is good. Make the decision today to put God first. Make the decision today to spend the rest of your life living and being the best person you can be. Understand that anyone who turns their back on God for any reason, idols, adultery, theft and even greed, will not enter into heaven or have the kingdom of God. If you want the kingdom of God, let your heart not be troubled, open it and accept the Lord, then make the decision to live with God at the forefront of everything that you do.

Conclusion:

Life is what you make it. It has its ups and down. Do not go through each day living your life worrying about what could have been or what will be. Do not give the devil power by entertaining any of his actions in your thoughts. Don't let others drive you crazy by handing them the keys. Don't let people get on your nerves by laying your nerves down for them. Understand that God has a plan for your life. He has given you a vision and a purpose. You have the vision. Act on it. Believe it. Relish in it. Remember to keep God first in everything that you do and everything else will fall into place. Just have faith and believe in him, believe in you and you will receive the blessings of the Lord and the favor of God.

Made in the USA
San Bernardino, CA
08 August 2016